Jan Morris, who was born in 1925, divides her time between her library-house in North Wales, her *dacha* in the Black Mountains of South Wales, and travel abroad. This is her second volume of autobiography, the first, *Conundrum*, having described her mid-life change of sexual role. Her other books include the *Pax Britannica* trilogy about the British Empire, studies of Wales, Venice, Oxford, Manhattan and Hong Kong, six volumes of collected travel essays and a novel, *Last Letters from Hav*, which was shortlisted for the Booker Prize in 1985. She edited the *Oxford Book of Oxford*, is now writing a book about Sydney, and next year will be editing the collected travel writings of Virginia Woolf.

Pleasures
of a Tangled Life
JAN MORRIS

ARROW BOOKS

Arrow Books Limited
20 Vauxhall Bridge Road, London SW1V 2SA

An imprint of Random Century Group

London Melbourne Sydney Auckland Johannesburg
and agencies throughout the world

First published in Great Britain in 1989 by Barrie & Jenkins Ltd

Arrow edition 1990

Typeset by Input Typesetting Ltd, London

Printed and bound in Great Britain by
The Guernsey Press Co Ltd, Guernsey, Channel Islands.

ISBN 0 099 80310 0

Contents

To the best of all my Pleasures:
My love and my children,
their *loves* and *their* children

1
Prologue:
On Pleasures in Principle

When Pluto and Socrates (to start at the top) reached a compromise on their views about the nature of the Good, they decided that while stern Intelligence must play a predominant part in it, sensual Pleasure came an important second. Evolutionists, if indeed they see a virtue to existence, might put it the other way round. The pursuit of pleasure is so powerful an instinct that it far outstrips any effect of thought upon the survival and development of the species. If it were not for the pleasure of food and drink, we would starve. If it were not for the pleasure of sex, we would die out. If it were not that sleeping is enjoyable, we would waste away from exhaustion, and if defecation were not, on the whole, quite a happy experience all our systems would dysfunction. I am not quite sure why sneezing and yawning have been made such fun, but I am sure physiologists know, and as to the aesthetic pleasures, the pleasures of art and nature, perhaps if it were not for their calming influence we might all have annihilated each other by now.

So pleasures are not to be scoffed at. They may be no more than intermissions from pain, as some depressing theorists maintain, but they must be taken seriously. Even the severest Puritan ate turkey dinner at Thanksgiving, even the dourest Stalinist knew that an occasional visit to the cinema improved tractor production, and now and then it still crosses political minds that really the only purpose of statesmanship is to ensure the people's pleasures. Freudian psychoanalysts speak of The Pleasure Theory, one of the less arcane of their keys to human understanding. Competitive mathematicians around the world are reducing pleasures into scientific formulae, and there is a device for measuring them, called a hedonometer.

I told an acquaintance of mine that I was writing a book about

Pleasure. 'What a coincidence,' she said, 'my husband is writing one about Forgiveness.' My purpose, though, is altogether less elevated than his. He is setting out to demonstrate, I have no doubt, the spiritual, psychological and theological meaning of forgiveness. I am merely out to show once more, by the examples of my own life and taste, out of my own peculiar circumstances, what a pleasure pleasures are.

Peculiar circumstances, however, doubtless lead to peculiar satisfactions, and this book is really a species of autobiography. I wrote an earlier memoir, *Conundrum*, which was chiefly about the doubts and problems of sexual confusion. That confusion having been settled, I thought I would now write the obverse, so to speak – a companion book simply about the happy side of my life. I would dismiss the tangled past, celebrate the unencumbered present. However, the more I thought about the things that gave me pleasure, the more it dawned upon me how specific they must be to my particular sensibility. There was a time when, new to life as a woman, I tried to forget that I had ever lived as a man, but it had grown on me over the years that this was not only intellectually dishonest, but actually rather dull of me. Now I realized I enjoyed the present largely in reflection to the past; the tangle that was part of me, whether I liked it or not; mine were pleasures experienced by a traveller across strange frontiers, and they were unlikely to work in quite the way other people's pleasures worked.

They include, indeed, many pleasures ordinary enough, pleasures generic and particular, of place and of fancy, sustained and momentary pleasures, pleasures tart and pleasures rather sickly, pleasures of eating, reading, listening to music and being Welsh. Their emblematic centre-piece, however, is a pleasure only I can have. It concerns a long-dead Admiral, Lord Fisher of Kilverstone, with whom I have enjoyed for many years an imaginary, complex, highly enjoyable, and so far as he is concerned entirely posthumous affair. I love this old champion, but in an ambiguous way: for a while one half of my being wishes to be cherished by him, somewhere in the other half I find lurking a residual wish to *be* him. Thus I see, in the pleasure Fisher gives me, a paradigm of my particular condition, and a kind of crystallization too, since I can pin it down to specific emotions, of the pleasure that the world in general gives me in the second half of my life; pleasure which, like my life itself, seems to be at bottom a yearning for unity – 'the desire and pursuit of the whole.'

But of course much of what I enjoy everyone else enjoys too, and like most autobiographies this book tends to hark back overtly or allusively to the pleasures of youth. I remember saying to a friend, during the Second World War, that I hoped to die before I was forty. Beyond that life-span, it seemed to me then, pleasures surely faded. The spring would go out of life, physically and figuratively, and the world would lose some of its mystery and surprise. Spring of step and spring of season, surprise, mystery, pleasure itself – I thought of them all as more or less synonymous, and did not much relish life without them.

In some ways I was right. It is idle to pretend that the world feels as fresh when you are sixty as it does when you are twenty-one. You have seen too much of it. Not only do its astonishments come more rarely, and its puzzles less intriguingly, but scepticism has almost certainly set in. Youth is gullible, and out of the readiness to believe comes much of its pleasure and its poetry. Few conversations, at any time of life, are more stimulating, more spontaneous and more genuinely original than those long ridiculous talks we all have, when we are very young, late at night about the meaning of life.

Besides, the command of comparisons which develops with age is, while no doubt good for the mind, somewhat numbing for the emotions. It is a wonderful thing to be able to look at an Italian cathedral and recognize the classical influences upon its Gothic, but it is still more wonderful to look at it altogether unaware, altogether open to its fascination. Literature is more thrilling before critical relativity arises; the worst of wine, in the early years of one's life, is better than the best towards the end; and as to your first love, earnestly though you may deny it to later partners, and even to yourself, nothing will ever really match its ecstacy, laced as it is likely to have been with reckless innocence.

For it is youth's innocent recklessness that counts. All the pleasures that are best enjoyed without fuss, without reservation, are

11

best indulged when you are young – taking chances, having affairs, making abrupt departures or unannounced arrivals. The gesture of risking everything upon an instant decision, so proper and exhilarating in youth, presently comes to feel anachronistic, like driving a sports car too dashing for you. Even swank, a forgiveable self-indulgence in one's teens, twenties and at a pinch thirties, mutates into ostentation with middle age.

Responsibility must share the blame – the older we get, the more we have to think of others. The imperceptibly approaching prospect of death, too, while in some it makes for frenzied hedonism ('If I were you,' said a colleague to the writer John Cheever, when he gave up alcohol in his sixties, 'I'd have gone out loaded.') probably in most of us consciously or unconsciously blunts the edge of pleasure. Chiefly, however, in my opinion, it is simply the accretion of experience, like a film over a lens, that dullens so many pleasures with age, and this paradox is certainly reflected in the pages of my book. As the years have passed I have myself learned to distinguish (I think) between spandrel and springer, I prefer Grand Cru to a Petit Chablis any day, I have very strong feelings about commas and marmalade and I have boxed the sexual compass. All this is satisfying, testifying as it does at least to a lifetime of varied purpose, but the satisfaction is inescapably tempered by a loss of naïvety. I have to work a little harder, to be surpised and excited. Often when the frisson does come I feel it not as an emotion of the present, but as a happy echo of the past, and even the most immediate of my pleasures are partly the pleasures of evocation – with comparison, complacency, complaint and jejune philosophy, the running theme of memoir.

Not that I care. I have been struck lately by a remarkably increasing prevalence of coincidence in my affairs, in matters great and small, and this I take to be confirmation of my instinct that all things are trying to be one. I have come to believe that the chief purpose of life is conciliation, and just as I have tried to concile male and female within myself, so I enjoy mingling the indulgences of youth and age. 'I don't think you need worry,' said my friend solicitously – he was seeing me off on a troop train – when I told him of my reluctance to live too long. 'You're just the type to get killed.' But

I wasn't, and this turned out to be a pleasure in itself, for later I changed my mind about dying young.

2
As to Sex

As to sex, the original pleasure, I cannot recommend too highly the advantages of androgyny.

At the time in the middle of my life when I was passing from one gender to the other, I was difficult to identify either as male or female. I might have been one or the other, or both, or neither. I knew it was only a temporary condition, and while it led to embarrassments now and then, it was often undeniably amusing. At a time of sexual indeterminacy, I found myself entertained as never before or since, because I discovered that both men and women, far from being repelled by my equivocal state, were intrigued and even attracted by it.

It was like being a star. Famous actors and actresses, they say, find themselves treated by their fans with a curious intimacy, as if by their very celebrity they have relinquished any private identity, and become universal relatives. So it was with me. Laying claim, as it must have seemed, to no recognizable sexual status, sometimes seizing, sometimes discarding the prerogatives of either gender, I was evidently amenable to all. Men and women equally confided in me, made moderate advances, and clearly felt neither threatened nor patronized. When after a few years my problems of gender mercifully found their resolution, I rather missed the sense of ubiquitous passport that the androgynous state had given me.

This was sex only of the most slanting and superficial kind – sex by allusion, by ellipsis. The experience nevertheless made me feel that perhaps there was in the world at large, as there certainly was in me, an innate ennui with the whole system of progeneration. If people felt relieved to venture beyond the usual peripheries of male and female, did it perhaps mean that all sexual orthodoxies, after so many million years of them, were becoming a bit of a bore?

I have always thought the physical pleasures of sex less than satisfying. They are not very subtle, after all. Birds do them, bees do them, and their only purpose is to encourage the reproductive urge. They seem to me not much more interesting than the business of eating; and actually mankind, in trying to make both pleasures more rewarding, has advanced much further with its cuisine than with its copulation – who could deny that a really good cookbook is intellectually more adventurous than the Kamasutra? One can hardly call sex fastidious, either. Children often avert their eyes in disgust when a particularly lubricious kiss is portrayed on a television screen, and to a man like George Orwell, who thought the handshake an unhygienic act, the coupling of bodies must have seemed a messy horror.

I myself do not find the act distasteful. Apart from its elemental enjoyment, which even Orwell must have recognized, at its best it seems to me to display the functional beauty of a scientific solution, or perhaps more appositely of a well-maintained engine – smooth, polished, the two frames designed and machined for one another as a piston couples with a cylinder. Male and female God made them, we are assured, and male and female too, long ago, engineers designated their nuts and bolts.

Indeed sex is more elegantly conducted by human beings than by many other creatures of the animal kingdom. Cats, dogs, birds, all function in far more ungainly ways. This is a surprise to me, for I have always thought mankind among the least comely of the beasts, so awkward of posture, so uninviting of texture. How could anyone prefer, I have frequently asked myself, the bare bony form of a human, male or female, to the perfection of a feline, whether thrillingly predatory in the shape of a cheetah, or voluptuously tantalizing in that of my own preference, an Abyssinian cat?

Not that I have any carnal knowledge of cats. I view with suspicion the notion of miscegenation between species. It is certainly not by any evolutionary error that the union of man and goat, for instance, is consummated only in myth, and I do not myself pine for the cross-bred chimerical world of centaurs, Pans or Pegasuses. On the other hand I can see no moral objection to sexual attraction of any kind, if it does no harm to third parties – only a dullard could see sexual beauty in one sex only, or for that matter species. Advertising people go further, and call cars or telephones sexy, and for myself it is many years since I realized that I found the attractions of the city of Venice not merely sensual, but actually sexual.

I am also unreliable about incest. In this of course I am not alone. Gilbert Murray the classicist, asked once if he was interested in incest, replied simply: 'Only in a general way.' I have no detailed experience of the matter either, and I certainly do not claim, as some cultures have, that meticulous incestry can produce superior beings – on the whole it did not seem to work too well among the ruling chieftains of Polynesia, whose taboo upon incest unfortunately applied to everyone except themselves. I am simply struck by the ideal nature of the practice. Blood love is the purest of loves, the love one is born to, so in principle what could be more beautiful than to seal it with the God-given gesture of physical union? If we are to believe Giraldus Cambrensis, the twelfth-century chronicler of Wales, we in Wales have always taken a relaxed view of incest. Only a year or two ago an elderly and widowed near-neighbour of mine, found guilty of sexual relations with his unmarried daughter, was sent to prison for it: but I was not alone in thinking it a mean-spirited response to a primitive expression of affection which was certainly genetically misguided, but which far from being the cruel abuse of one by the other, undoubtedly brought comfort to them both.

Particularly graceful, it seems to me, is the notion of love in all its forms between brother and sister, a variety of forbidden sex in which artists, writers and myth-makers down the ages have seen a poignant majesty. I used to express the hope, not very seriously, that my daughter would marry one of my sons – they were made for each other, I thought. Having declared this outrageous whim one day to an American guest, I introduced him to the two children (who have long since, I hasten to add, made more ordinary arrangements of their own). He looked from one to the other in benevolent appraisal. 'Ah yes,' he said, 'the young intended.'

Actually all the best sex, in my view, aspires to the condition of incest. Brothers and sisters we all become, if we love each other deep and long enough. I have lived with one partner for nearly forty years, through a greater permutation of sexual relationship

16

than a Grecian fabulist could conceive, and out of it all I have drawn the conclusion that the ultimate object of sex is not physical after all, but spiritual – beyond the production of children, the sealing of profounder unions. If evolution decreed that sex must be a pleasure to ensure the continuity of the species, a higher will conceived it more sacramentally, and its ultimate delight is nothing less than a glimpse of that final unity, the infinite.

It may be the only glimpse we get, and is hard to imagine sometimes. That corpulent couple in the dining-room, so protuberant that one would think it difficult for them to kiss, let alone to copulate – he in his thick serge waistcoated suit, smoking a cigar, she so primped of hair, so loudly bangled, so layered with makeup, the two of them steadily working, scarcely exchanging a word, through the heavy courses of their dinner – is it conceivable that, when they go upstairs to their room, they are this very evening to be afforded the momentary vision of the unimaginable that is sex's truest meaning? Certainly it is. We all feel it, everyone one of us, even those whose approach to sex is most vulgar. We may think it merely the crowning of bodily urges, but it is also an intimation of the divine.

For myself I find it more moving, on the whole, without the bodily functions at all – for the gods have so arranged things that the symbolism of sex can be exerted without the practicalities. For me some of its most profoundly stirring episodes have not been in bed at all, but have been moments of sudden revelation in the course of everyday life. Sometimes in moments of pity I have felt this shaft of truth, sometimes in a meeting or a parting, and sometimes, as I am feeling it at this instant, simply watching the person who is dearest to me in life sewing, dark glasses on the end of her nose, mouth pursed in concentration, at the next table of the French hotel terrace upon which I am writing.

And sometimes, as we all do, I have experienced it in a transient flash of communication with a perfect stranger. I was once in the Pump Room at Bath during the morning performance of the old Pump Room Trio, a combo of piano, violin and cello, middle-aged and enthusiastic, which specialized in properly Pump Room music like *Chanson d'Amour* or *Rustle of Spring* – I was listening spellbound to this music when I felt the unmistakable pull of someone else's attention. I looked around to meet the eyes of a man I took to be

17

a foreigner, and in his look I recognized not only precisely the same responses to the music as my own, touched and affectionate, but also the instant recognition of our unity before God – sex corporeal, sex spiritual, sex symbolical, all at the same time. In that brief moment I could have talked in tongues, if it had not been for *Pale Hands I Loved* behind the potted plants.

Even sex is relative, anyway. I first went to Venice as a subaltern in a British armoured regiment, and was billeted in a house on Giudecca with a fellow-officer. Thirty years later, as a middle-aged woman, I was back in the city making a television documentary, and thought it would be amusing to film the very same house. It had been turned into a school, though, and a gardener at the gate said that photography would most certainly not be permitted. What a pity, said I – years ago I had myself lived in the house, and I retained most happy memories of it. At once the gardener, good Italian that he was, put all things in perspective. 'Ah, signora,' he charmingly exclaimed, 'of course, of course – I remember you well!'

3
My House

Friends sometimes think excessive the pleasure I get from my house in North Wales, which is called Trefan Morys partly after the ancient estate that surrounds it, and partly after me. I love it above all inanimate objects, and above a good many animate ones too. I love it incessantly. When I am at home I wander around its rooms gloatingly; when I am away I lie in my hotel dreaming of it. If people show me pictures of their children, I show them pictures of my house, and there is nothing on earth I would swap it for, except possibly something by Giorgione.

Freudian amateurs, which friends so often are, find this preoccupation unnatural. It has a psycho-obsessive ring, they say. It shows a womb-longing – even a death-wish they sometimes add, especially when they learn that my gravestone already stands in a corner of my library. It is a kind of fetish, one might as well be in love with a washing-machine, or a stamp collection. But I see my passion in a different way. I love the house not just as a thing, but as a concentration of emotions and sensations, contained within a receptacle which in its style, its stance, its materials, its degree of grandeur and its position on the map, exactly represents all that I have most cherished or coveted in life.

The house is not at all large, luxurious or spectacular; yet the Sultan of Brunei could not build it, for it is infinitely more than the sum of its own modest parts. In my mind anyway it is almost a metaphysical house, and Fate indeed chose it for me, though only at the third attempt. Two other houses, over the years, I have displayed to people with a mystic confidence as the final home infallibly decreed for me. One I never did acquire, one I sold; only then did destiny look up the back lane to Trefan Morys.

It consists in essence simply of two living-rooms, one above the other, each about forty feet long. Both are full of books, and there is a little suite of functional chambers on two floors at one end, linked by a spiral staircase. The building was the stable-block of my family house (number two on the destiny roster, which I sold in the 1970s), and long ago our children used to light bonfires on its cobbled floors. It was built in 1774, of massively rough-hewn local stone, and has a small slate-strewn yard outside, with a wild garden intended to suggest the bottom of a wood. On its roof is a white cupola, sheltering the television aerial and supporting a weathervane which displays, besides my initials, the points of the compass half in Welsh, half in English: E and W for east and west, G and D for *gogledd* and *de*.

Passers-by, to be honest, do not much notice my house. There are many such buildings in Wales, and standing as it does on an unnoticeable lane among a clutter of farm buildings old and new, Trefan Morys looks nothing special. If I happen to see strangers walking by, though, all too often I grab them, shove a glass of wine in their hands and lure them inside; and then almost invariably, particularly if they are Welsh, some magic of the place seizes them too, and they leave Trefan Morys nearly as besotted as I am.

This is because they recognize a numen to the old structure. There is a kind of radiance to it, and it arises I am sure because generations of good people, harmless creatures and benevolent things have been happy and diligent in the house. There were the woodmen, for instance, who fashioned its timbers with such care from the oak woods down by the river – each beam marked with its number still, and with the initials of my eighteenth-century predecessor at Trefan, the Reverend Isaiah Hughes, a bigoted churchman but an enlightened improver of properties. There were the stonemasons who miraculously heaved its cyclopean blocks one on top of another. There were the carpenters who built its simple pine staircase, and the glaziers who created its many-paned chapel-like windows. There were the stable-hands who, for so many decades before me, lived in the building above their horses – excellent men without doubt, who laughed a lot up there, and entertained themselves merrily with beer and stable-songs.

Owls inhabited the place for many years, and I have commemorated them with an engraved window. Bats, mice, sundry birds, multitudinous insects and a couple of cats share it not always entirely harmoniously now. There is a slightly over-squashy and claw-frayed sofa, and models of three local schooners, made for me over the years by Mr Bertie Japheth of Trefor, are mounted on cross-beams above – an arrangement I thought unique until I noticed the Venetian galley in Carpaccio's picture of St Jerome. Silent in their white cases stand those benign old friends, my books, and through the rooms there often sounds the ancient and glorious language of the Welsh.

In the middle of it all, at the end of it, and in a mystical way, I like to think, at the beginning of it too, there stand I, owner and lover of the place.

As you see it is a complex pleasure, but then all the best ones are, and in one sense my friends are right. Not only do I immensely admire my house and all it stands for, but I have come to cherish it in a distinctly erotic way. I feel myself in intimate physical rapport with its old oak, and frequently talk lovingly to its walls and empty spaces. When I come back to it after a long journey, opening with its big eighteenth-century key its crooked blue-painted front door – when I enter its presence once again I experience more than mere relief or comfort, but something undeniably akin to lechery.

Now there *is* something for the Freudians! But more neurotic still, you may think, is my last thought about Trefan Morys: that if on the one hand I love my house more salaciously than I should, on the other my house, I long ago came to realize, is perfectly infatuated with me.

4

The Taste for Anarchy

One intemperate morning on Kharkov airport, in the Ukraine, I experienced a glorious moment of liberation. We had been hanging about for hours, through delay after delay in the bitterly cold and uninviting waiting-room, fobbed off by supercilious airline employees, brushed aside by boorish officials, until at last the patience of my Soviet fellow-passengers expired. They found a boarding-ramp, pushed it on to the tarmac, opened the aircraft door for themselves, and brushing aside the horrified stewardesses, plumped themselves in their seats and called for vodka. I followed in their wake rejoicing, feeling as though we had stormed all life's varied Kremlins.

I am an anarchist at heart – an anarchist *manquée*, because I lack the courage fully to honour my convictions, but one who temperamentally prefers the criminal to the cop, the prisoner to the guard, and who sees as the ultimate political ideal the abolition of all authority. I resent the whole apparatus of hierarchy that William Cobbett used to call 'The Thing'. The less government the better, for my money, the fewer bureaucrats, the fewer rules. The American founding fathers took a step in the anarchist direction, when they declared that government must have the consent of the governed – that American citizens were nobody's subjects but their own. Unfortunately the instinct of the British leads them in precisely the opposite direction. Legally they are still the subjects of Her Majesty the Queen, and psychologically they are profoundly dependent upon official order and regulation. Their very eccentricites are safety valves, giving a reassuring impression of individuality, and you have only to read a London newspaper, or listen to the radio news, to realize how obsessed they are by matters of government. I hope it is the Welsh in me that has released me from these instincts, and made the taste for anarchy one of my abiding entertainments.

How I detest, as a matter of enjoyable principle, all aspects and symptoms of authority, anywhere in the world: the concept of school prefects, the sarcasm of teachers, the arrogance of customs officials, the rudeness of post office assistants, the self-satisfaction of Social Security clerks, the sanctimony of magistrates, the busy-bodiness of inspectors, the smugness of prison warders, the insolence of censors, the bossiness of security men, the self-importance of Cabinet Ministers, the hypocrisy of policemen, the general impertinence of all kinds of second-rate, overblown, swollen-headed and humourless petty jacks-in-office! It is a positive pleasure to dislike them so, and to feel that at least life has spared me the degradation of being set in authority over anyone else. The only authority I have ever really admired – even enjoyed – was that of the British Army, which in my day at least was perceptibly tinged with self-amusement. The most traditionally terrifying of regimental sergeant-majors, whose bawls could send a shiver down a mass-murderer's spine, when dealing with innocent recruits generally betrayed a fatherly concern behind the fury, and were very jovial if met in pubs off-duty. For the rest, it is no good protesting to me that there are decent magistrates, modest Ministers, helpful post office workers and even kindly cops: so far as I am concerned, at least when writing essays, they have one and all sold themselves to the devil.

It is the presumptuousness of authority that most makes my blood boil. 'Somebody has to do it,' they say, and quite rightly: but why does it always have to be *them*? Why do they never exert their discipline apologetically or diffidently? How have they persuaded themselves, as they sit in their ridiculous wigs on the bench, that they are really better people than the poor wretches in the dock? It has been a regular practice of my life to attend courts of law, wherever I go in the world: chiefly of course for professional reasons, because they offer such insights into the social, political and moral condition of a place, but partly for the pure pleasure of offering the accused a smile of sympathy, while eyeing judges, court clerks and self-satisfied barristers with a deliberate look of mordant ridicule – there is nothing they can do, even in countries of the most absolute despotism, to ban a middle-aged lady from their courts because of the expression on her face.

Above all I like to sneer at the English law. It is not of course the worst – very far from it – but it is the most pompous. It seems to have arrogated to itself, as the centuries have passed, delusions of divine sovereignty, inherited from the monarchy itself. In other countries an accused malefactor faces a dispute with his peers. In America it is The People that accuses him, elsewhere it is The Republic. In Sweden he sits on a level with his judges, talking to them man to man. In the Soviet Union at least they call him comrade. In India I have seen accused felons sleeping in the dock with their heads on their warders' shoulders. Even in Scotland judges sometimes manage to make one feel that they are merely advocates within a family feud. But in England that ass the Law, dressed up preposterously in trappings not of arbitration, but of overbearing authority, acts on behalf of Her Majesty the Queen in accusing one of her Subjects, and seems to suppose that we must all treat it with a semi-superstitious awe. I like to fantasize some-times, as I watch those puffed-up judges, slimy QCs and loveless policemen, that suddenly by some miracle they are all stripped of their silly fineries, and are left gesturing there utterly in the nude, paunches, pimples and all.

Another complacent community I like cocking a snook at is the Family of Science. I have no faith in it at all, and delight in ridiculing its presumptious dogmas. Peter Fleming wrote a fanciful essay once in which, having declared to a stranger on a train his belief in a flat earth, he was disconcerted to discover that he had been addressing the Astronomer Royal. I would not have been in the least put out, having long ago reached the conclusion that in great matters at least astronomers, like most scientists, are probably wrong. I would not claim that the earth was flat, now that we have all seen its curvature for ourselves, but it amuses me to propagate the view that our planet is the only single body in the entire universe that sustains life. Why not? It is as least as likely as any other hypothesis, in a field so dominated by improbabilities, and if people ask me how in that case I can believe in UFOs, I say they have emerged from the earth's bowels through the volcanic vents of the ocean floor.

I see no conclusive evidence for the fact of evolution. Keble used to say that when God made the rocks he made the fossils in them, and the explanation seems to me perfectly acceptable. Whoever thought of arranging for the crab called *Lybia tesselata* to use stinging sea-anemones as weapons, or organized the residence of roundworms within the pharyngeal glands of ants, or taught the termite *apicotermes gurgulifex* to punch precisely regular ventilation slits in the nest it makes from its own excrement, or so fixed things that during an eclipse of the sun the circumference of the moon, seen from the earth, exactly fits the circumference of the sun – whoever evolved these virtuoso displays of caprice might just as well have thought it entertaining to build the relics of a few imaginary monsters into the sandstone.

It may perhaps be that the whole of our universe, from the atom to the most distant galaxy, constitutes a single parasite within the being of some inconceivably gigantic organism, or perhaps a globule within its bloodstream. More probably, though (and this is what I would say to the Astronomer Royal, if *I* met him on the train), we are all the victims, or perhaps the beneficiaries, of a divine hoax. Why else would anybody invent the duckbilled platypus? Science offers no answers to the voice of reason.

Often authority skulks underground, making it more unlikeable still, and I myself had a curious brush with that kind in Panama some years ago. I had been given an introduction to Colonel Manuel Noriega, then chief of the security police, later to become Head of State and to be accused by the United States of drug dealing. I was told to present myself at his downtown bunker, and made my way there through successive rings of checkpoints, barbed wire, electronic surveillance devices and military orderlies. Finally I found myself within the colonel's innermost headquarters, the real focus of power in Panama.

Noriega never turned up. I was left to myself, until I had exhausted the experience, to wander around his windowless air-conditioned suite, inspecting its displays of office. Except for the fact that through loudspeakers came the hymns and exhortations of an evangelical radio station called *The Bright Sounds of Inspiration*, it was like looking at the bedroom of an over-indulged adolescent. The chrome and white leather objects, the pictures of girls and the cocktail cabinets, were balanced by guns, books about military intelligence, flickering closed-circuit screens and a huge picture of the colonel parachuting out of an aeroplane. We are ruled by children, I thought to myself as I looked at all this, and of course it's true: the very instinct of authority is an instinct of immaturity, well worth the pleasure of laughing at, whenever practicable, just to cut it down to size.

Though Noriega failed to keep his appointment that day, I was told recently that Panamanian gossip had me, as the saying is, establishing a relationship with him after my visit to his bunker. Some relationship that would have been! I would have driven him mad with mockery. *Bright Sounds of Inspiration* indeed.

5

The Best Meal in the World

Long ago I identified The Best Meal in the World – the best meal, that is, of the kind that restaurant guides like to call an *experience*, or even a *happening*. Having enjoyed over the years a succession of meals which I wrongly thought were the best imaginable, I tracked it down definitively to Stockholm, Sweden, on a Sunday lunchtime shortly before Christmas.

I got there the day before, and found the city all celebration, all candles on its head. It dazzled me with its festivity. Out from their quays with siren-toots the little pleasure steamers sailed one by one, bedecked with lights and tinsel, taking happy office parties on cruises through the archipelago. Music rang perpetually above the outdoor skating rink, where young and old swooped and staggered beneath the floodlights, while all along the wharves suburban burghers and their wives, attended by burbling children, loaded their Volvos with Christmas trees from waterfront vendors.

The shops were decorated in the fastidious Swedish way, opulent but not bloated, but were attended by a wild host of Christmas elves; elves animate and inanimate, elves plump and elves skinny, mechanically nodding or breathing elves, winking elves and dancing elves and elves sometimes flat on their backs asleep. In windows everywhere, high and low, electric candelabra cheerfully shone. Here and there a pungent alcoholic smell attracted me, and upon payment of a few kronor a gloved hand reached out of a dark street-stall, like a messenger from the forest, to hand me a steaming cup of glogg, the spicy mulled wine of the Swedes.

There were Lappish-looking people around, with high cheeks, slant eyes and fur-lined boots. There were gaunt elderly aristocrats in astrakhan hats. Rosy girls ate ice-creams in café windows, and old men in boats pottered around the ice-strewn harbour fishing.

27

Half-frigid but ever dauntless, as the sun went down, the poor sentries stood in their boxes outside the empty royal palace, or marched stiffly up and down the cobbled streets behind, while from the great gilded church of Storkyrkan nearby came the festive music of an organ.

Was it a dream? Brrr . . . it was not. Bitter blew the sea winds, slippery with snow were the lanes of the Old City, and there were times when I found myself running the last few yards to the comfort of the coffee-shop. But then that seemed to me the glory of the moment – that so grand a city should be celebrating so merrily in the December gloom of the north.

Sunday dawned brilliant. The Best Meal was drawing close, but first I had to honour an old Stockholm tradition, and go out to Skansen on the ferry: through the icy harbour, past the big night boat from Helsinki, leaving the spires and gabled houses of the Old City like an antique engraving behind.

Skansen is Stockholm's celebrated and beloved folk museum, a large hilly park a mile or two from the centre of town, in which old buildings of all sorts have been lovingly reconstructed, indigenous animals and birds are cherished, and Swedishness in a generic kind reaches a conservational apogee. It is a marvellous place always, but on my particular Sunday it was magical, for half Stockholm was out there for the Skansen Christmas bazaar, a rambling assemblage of stalls offering all sorts of Christmassy Scandinavian objects – straw goats, and hats with ear-flaps, and little lanterns, and painted wooden horses, and sheepskins, and furry boots, and heart-shaped sweetmeats. People wearing old Swedish costume attended the stalls, the women in embroidered caps and voluminous skirts, the men in jerkins and quaint hats, and now and then a thin Swedish-style Santa Claus stalked through, his reindeer impersonated by a colleague bent double beneath a blanket and crowned with a pair of horns.

Around the edge of the bazaar things were livelier still. There the glogg flowed, and men were grilling herrings on racks over open fires. A hundred thousand Swedish ducks congregated with confident quacks at the edge of their pond, demanding titbits, and all over the place adorable bundled children were to be seen petting squirrels or in eye-to-eye confrontation with lugubrious elks. High on a roof-top four storks looked down upon the goings-on: into the wooden church beyond the lake an elderly blind couple, well-wrapped, tapped their way towards the carol concert.

I was getting hungry now. It was the smell of the glogg and the grilled herrings that did it, but it was nearly lunch-time anyway. The light was already beginning to fade, but the Best Meal lasts all afternoon, so I had plenty of time to walk back to town along the hilariously skiddy sidewalks beneath the big bare trees. Along the waterfront I went, and past the statue of Charles XII the conqueror pointing his sword peremptorily towards Leningrad, until I stood in the lee of the Stockholm Royal Opera House, flambeaus flaring bravely in the wind along its high parapet. Since 1895 the Operakallaren on its ground floor has been the most celebrated restaurant in Sweden, and for many years it has served the most famous of all the world's smorgasbords. This magnificent repast is what I had come to Stockholm for.

They serve it every day at the Operakallaren, but Sunday is the best day because then, by a long-established custom, Stockholmers like to go there *en famille*; and a Sunday shortly before Christmas is best of all, for under the blessing of St Lucia one may then share the pleasures of the Swedes at their most genial, their most generous and (I choose my words carefully, for they are an abstemious people) their least ungluttonous.

The ambiance of the meal was tremendous. The great baroque dining-room is decorated with a series of mythological paintings which were thought in the 1890s to be downright indecent, but now just seem amiably nubile, and it looks out through big windows to the harbour and the palace. On that Sunday the victuals were displayed on a gigantic table in the middle, and above them, just for Christmas, was suspended a large gingerbread model of the Opera House itself. The light of the chandeliers was subdued, the warmth was palpable, the head waiter who showed me so courteously to my table looked like a Baltic duke.

White, white was my table-cloth, velvety my chair, fastidiously polished the cutlery, and before I got any further here before me was my glass of the Operakallaren's own aquavit, Stenborgare,

29

named for an eigtheenth-century opera singer, subtly flavoured
with fennel and aniseed, and available nowhere else. *Skoll!* Like
aromatic fire it went down, and I was ready in body and spirit for
The Best Meal in the World.

It was a feast of feasts, not only of food, but of life and sociability
too. The Swedes are famously reserved, but once their shyness is
broached they are the most companionable of people, and as I
lined up plate in hand for nourishment kindly voices guided me
towards the most interesting pickled herring, explained to me the
history of Stenborgare, introduced me to their mother-in-law Mrs
Andersson or abjured little Erik to stand up straight when addressing strangers.

Little Erik, actually, was standing up admirably straight already,
dressed as he was in his best suit, with a bow tie and a rather
uncomfortable collar, and his sister Eva was extremely smart in
blue check, and Mrs Andersson was a most elegant old dame, and
altogether my companions presented a splendid picture of plump
well-being and goodwill, as they urged me to shovel another portion
of elk-meat on to the corner of my plate.

Elk-meat, or Swedish caviare, or salmon from great ravaged
carcasses, or game, or berries, or cheeses, or cream, or prawns, or
pickles, or reindeer tongue – 'you can always come back for more,'
said Mrs Andersson encouragingly. I took her advice, too, for in
fact the food was not very filling, the afternoon was long, another
Stenborgare presently turned up from nowhere, and the conversation was delightfully digestive. 'Will you not have some cloudberr-
ies?' asked Eva in her most careful English, 'people like them very
much in Sweden.' And I did, I did.

So the hours passed, and soon it was pitch black outside the
windows, and the lights of the flambeaus were dancing and flickering in the dark. All was friendly, comfortable, decorous and ample.
As soon as one family of Anderssons left, another just as well-
dressed, just as smiling, was shown to its table. One salmon was
replaced by the next on the great smorgasbord table, elk succeeded
elk, shoals of herrings came and went. The head waiter, when at
last the time came for me to leave, no longer seemed like a head
waiter at all, or even a duke, but more like an old family friend. I

said goodbye to him almost nostalgically: by the nature of things, The Best Meal in the World can come but once a year.

6
On Music

The most boring moments of my life, almost bar none, have occurred during concerts. I have dreaded concerts always, except those in which my brother Gareth was playing a flute concerto, and in those I was half-paralysed with nerves on his behalf. Stuck there in a chair hour after hour, whether or not one likes the music, unable even to read a book, let alone make a cup of tea or whistle the melodies – the experience seems to me so dismal that when I was young I assumed everyone else in a concert audience to be as unhappy as I was. The poet Pope thought just the same, and believed people went to concerts only to be seen or to show off their enlightenment.

This predisposition meant that, although I came from an intensely musical family, for many years I took little pleasure in listening to music. It was the electronic revolution that changed everything. I did not possess a record-player until I was in my middle twenties, and it was only then that I realized music to be not a mere branch of the performing arts, but part of the cosmos – harmonies (or disharmonies) plucked out of the universal sounds, as one might take messages from the wind.

I recognized then that my dislike of concerts, dressed up as they all too often are in the trappings of show business and social decorum, was one of a kind with my dislike of organized religion. The absurd spectacle of a violinist pouring with sweat because he is buttoned up in a boiled shirt seems to me one with the preposterous antics of High Anglican acolytes. Music, to my mind, is best enjoyed by oneself and in freedom, as one enjoys nature: and it is best left to linger, so that in later years I came to believe that the walls of houses should be impregnated with it, and made a habit of leaving the record-player on when there was nobody at home to hear. I recognize the extra element of excitement to a live performance, the electric tingle of risk and challenge, but still on balance I agree with Glen Gould, who thought public concerts had been superseded by recordings (just as I agree with Dr Johnson's dictum that the invention of printing rendered the lecture unnecessary).

Surely it must be a delight for Bach or Mozart, as they look down upon our sphere from St Cecilia's boudoir, to find that their music is portable. They thought it had to be played in churches and Margraves' salons, and could sound only if choristers and harpsi-chordists were assembled. Now they hear it carried from room to room of condominiums, or blaring suddenly from car windows. 'May we go back to the beginning again?' a patron would ask in the old days, 'Her Highness enjoyed it so much' – and with a rustling of pages, a creaking of music-stands, the flutter of dropped scores and anxious coughs from the back-row fiddles, back to the beginning they went. Nowadays, if you want to return not just to the beginning, but to the start of the second movement or the aria on page 7, the mere press of a compact disc button will take you instantly there.

Portable music is a nuisance to many people, I know, especially when expressed over gigantic transistors on beaches. I have often been embarrassed when, stopping the car for fuel and switching the engine off, I have found my own cassette music blaring fortissimo as any ghetto-blaster over the forecourt. Nevertheless much of my most pleasurable experience of music has been in the car; I cannot honestly pretend that I have managed to soak Beethoven into the steel and plastic of my Honda, but I have never felt closer to the true sources of art than I have been when driving to music.

This is because I can relate it not only to movement, but to landscape too – much more proper than any concert hall for the most evanescent of the arts. I have no ear for rock and roll, but I can imagine that it would be marvellously enhanced by high speeds on a motorway, while the plots and settings of operas being what they mostly are, their passions can only be heightened by the rush of wind, the passing of hill and mountain and the opportunity one is given, in the privacy of one's car, to join in the more accessible of their arias. I was pilloried once in Pseuds' Corner, an acerbic column in the London magazine *Private Eye*, for claiming to choose my cassette music according to my journey – I had nominated something from *Tosca*, as I remember, as background to the crossing of the Severn Bridge. I was not abashed by the sneer, however, and so assiduously indeed have come to relate my music to the passing scene that some parts of the world I associate ineradicably with particular themes.

For example when I drove for the first time down the coast of Yugoslavia, from Istria to Montenegro, I had just acquired a recording, by Vladimir Ashkenazy with the Philharmonia Orchestra, of one of Mozart's piano concertos, I forget which. The allegro movement of this piece contained a tremendously vivacious solo run, cascading from one end of the piano to the other, which was repeated several times and which absolutely suited, it seemed to me, the swashbuckling landscape of karst, sea and island through which my white BMW was sweeping. The combination did marvels for my spirits, and I drove down that magnificent highway repeatedly playing the tape, laughing and singing all the way. In the course of the journey I gave a lift to a frail and elderly Montenegrin traveller, wizard-like with stick and black coat, and when towards the end of the journey, Mr Ashkenazy still playing, in the delight of my mood I narrowly escaped head-on collision with a convoy of Yugoslav armoured cars, this aged worthy seemed to find it just as funny as I did – so intoxicating, I like to think, was the mix of place, sound and horsepower.

Similarly I never go down the Grand Canal without hearing Mendelssohn in my mind. I had a recording of his Italian Symphony in the days when I lived in an apartment above the canal, and I knew that he had written it after his own first visit to Venice. Sailing along that waterway for the first time, he said, made him feel like a prince coming into his inheritance, and whenever I go back to Venice precisely the same emotions are stirred in me by the memory of his music – such a happy strut and confidence, such a fine beat and richness of orchestration, that I too feel the city to be mine. Not, of course, that this sensation is necessarily musical. At the end of the Second World War it was often my duty to conduct visiting Allied generals into Venice, and Mendelssohnian without benefit of symphony at all was the expression of joyous wonder which irradiated even the most warlike of their faces as we chugged towards Rialto.

Perhaps they were thinking, like von Blücher in Paris, 'What a place to loot!', or perhaps for all their martial instincts they were hearing melodies of their own. Almost all of us, I suppose, have tunes in our heads – a distinguished conductor of my acquaintance, accused of making irritating swooshing and swishing noises with his mouth, said they weren't swooshing and swishing noises, they were the full score of Mahler's Ninth. Nothing is more marvellous than the apparently infinite number of tunes which the mental computer can store – thousands, I would guess, in almost every memory, and recoverable too by quoting the merest snatch of a Tallis motet, 'Knock 'Em In The Old Kent Road', 'Yellow Submarine' or a Havergal Brian symphony.

I am told that until his extreme old age, indeed, Havergal Brian heard most of his own music *only* in his head. Nobody had ever performed it. Surely this is music in *excelsis*, the very antithesis of music in the auditorium – music which exists only in the imagination, never having been brought down to earth with brass and catgut. I have some music of my own like that, but I hear it only when I look through a telescope at the planet Saturn. Gustav Holst heard symphonic sounds when he contemplated that heavenly object, but in my own case it is only a gentle pair of high-pitched hums, undulating sinuously one around the other, that reach and excite me across the divide.

7
Performers

I was sitting one day in a restaurant in Manhattan, concentrating on my lunch, when I heard the voice of a friend behind me. 'I want to introduce you to somebody, Jan' – and turning around, there beside my acquaintance I saw, holding out his hand to shake mine, Douglas Fairbanks Jnr.

The sight of him there took me aback. Not only did he look, though by then in his late seventies, astonishingly fit, youthful and handsome, but he also looked absolutely as I had known him vicariously all his life. He was not in the least diminished by his transition from costume drama to real life, from swashbuckle to lunch-time pleasantry. Nor, it seemed to me, had he aged at all since I had first wondered at his derring-do on the cinema screen forty or fifty years earlier. It was as though his persona had been established once and for all in my mind, so that neither time nor circumstance could shift it. I had similar feelings once when I saw Ginger Rogers, an elegant old lady, stepping down Madison Avenue with just the same verve as she had shown in the company of Fred Astaire a couple of generations before; and tapping my heels in irritation one day when my flight was delayed to await the boarding of an unnamed VIP, I was utterly mollified when Maria Callas swept towards the first-class compartment bestowing stupendously operatic smiles on one and all.

'Larry's lunching with me,' said Fairbanks. 'His back's giving him trouble, or he would have come over too. Give him a wave!' So I did wave to the frail stooped figure I now recognized at a table across the room, and when Olivier returned the greeting, in a bemused way, for he had not the slightest notion who I was, I saw in his gesture young Harry the King on Crispin Crispian's Day.

I seldom go to the theatre, so it is chiefly through television and the cinema that I have had the pleasure of getting to know my performers. There are scores that I have come to regard as friends without ever having met them. I have grown up with many of them, and when they die I read of it in the paper with a personal pang, frequently compounded by the fact that only from their brief obituaries do I first learn who they are.

For my favourites among those distant acquaintances are not the stars, but the myriad character actors, whose faces, gestures and voices are so much more familiar to us than their identities. They have enriched our lives in most peculiar ways. They have magically made us feel we know, as we know our own neighbours, cowboys and gangsters, villainous businessmen and comical surgeons, cops from across the world, Cockney sailors or American chorus girls – talking in every variety of English accent, springing from cultures remote indeed from our own, and introducing us to styles of thought and sense of humour that we might otherwise never have dreamed of.

Of course the performers have heightened everything with their craft. Even into camera acting is an artificial business. Nobody talks as slow as that really, few facial expressions are quite so revealing, Texans seldom speak Texan quite like Hollywood Texans and I have not for many years seen an English gentleman as gentlemanly as the small-part actors who wear the Old Etonian ties on television. By the nature of things character actors, in particular, tend towards caricature.

But anyway, we know the characters they play less intimately than the characters they are. We have watched them so often, those stalwarts of the screen, pretending to be so many different sorts of person, that long ago we learnt to see through their devices. I think with affection of a particular American actor, whose name I have never known, but whose every gesture is familiar to me, and whose face I can summon up at will – from the grave by now, I dare say. Grey-haired and distinguished, with rather protruding eyes and a resolutely cynical mouth, I have met him down the years as tycoon and army officer, as advertising executive and as senior police officer, in musicals and in heavy drama.

He is a very accomplished actor, and it is not through lack of skill that he fails to make me suspend my disbelief. It is simply that I know him too well. I can see him easily driving home from the studio after work, drinking dry martinis (he is of the martini age) beside the neighbours' tennis court, proud at his daughter's wedding or lining up to vote at a polling booth. I can even imagine him, urbane as ever, reminiscing with colleagues at the Hollywood home for retired actors – which must be peopled, indeed, with friends of mine just as well-remembered.

I find it sad to think that if I myself walked into that retirement home, and saw those acquaintances all around me (looking at old movies, I conjecture, or out-doing each other with press clippings) not one of them would recognize me. Ours is a one-way friendship. The Russian author Saltykov-Shchedrin, finding himself in his last years without a magazine to write for, said he had lost the one person he had ever loved, his reader. The screen actor can never acquire this sense of contact. His audience is numbered in millions, and he is seldom alone with any one of them, as Shchedrin felt himself alone with his subscriber.

I sense this poignancy always when, as happens now and then, I chance to see in the flesh one of those nameless and numberless actresses of television comedy, encountered in the underground, perhaps, or browsing in a bookshop. At first I think I really do know her. Who could she be? Is she a publisher, or a fellow-author? Did we meet on an aircraft, or at a literary festival somewhere? Like one of those nagging fragrances one cannot place, or a tune whose words we never quite remember, her presence tantalizes and disturbs me. Then with a touch of melancholy I realize that I know her only by proxy, through the medium of the screen. Some people in these circumstances introduce themselves anyway, and perhaps one should; I sometimes notice that if I chance to catch the woman's eye she will give me one of those closed-lip actress's smiles, turned up a little too resolutely at the corner of the mouth, as if she is dying to be recognized.

But it may be that performers want only to be known by their own kind. Their public is theory, but their colleagues are fact, and I dare say the incestuous self-indulgence of the Oscar and Emmy fandangos expresses their aspirations more truly than we suppose. The actress in the bookshop may smile in a stagey way at me, but

38

at the Equity meeting that evening she will doubtless be perfectly natural, and old age in the actors' home may come as a true release – life at last in the real world. Certainly when I was once taken to a Hollywood restaurant by Edmund Gwenn, himself one of the best-known of all character actors, the screen people who came one after the other to speak to him at our table seemed to me without guile or affectation, moving as they were among their peers and fellows. They semed quite ordinary then.

The same cannot be said, in my experience, of the supreme theatrical stars. They are the elect of our time, and they have been transformed by a fame beyond the dreams of earlier generations.

Some great actors seem to be permanently acting. It is their strength and their fascination. I interviewed Sybil Thorndike once, and felt that every syllable she uttered was as meticulously honed for meaning as it was for intonation. She suggested to me those moments, all too rare I fear, when I am quite consciously driving my car, concentrating on every gear-change instead of allowing half my mind to think of other things. Sometimes this is the glory of actors on stage, too: Olivier for instance, whose allure seems to me to come from the very deliberation of his performance, so calculated, so intoxicatingly false; or Gielgud, whose very phrase is a declaration of theatrical heritage – he once declaimed some lines of mine, in a commentary for a *son et lumière*, and I hardly recognized my own words, apotheosized as they were by his mellifluous perfection. Staginess becomes a triumph in playing of such stature, and one is transported not into another reality, but into the marvel of unreality itself.

Two celebrated English actors I have briefly encountered, however, enthralled me in quite a different way. I met Ralph Richardson at his splendid house overlooking Regent's Park, together with his tame rat and the motorbike upon which he had roared up to its front door just as I arrived myself. Never have I met a stranger man. He seemed to me less like an actor than some singular and tremendous grandee of the past, sitting in his town palace. It might easily have been Richardson himself, I thought, who had commissioned Nash to build the terraces that lined the park, and ran away into crescents, circles and parades across London. I could not make him out at all. Was he laughing at himself? His cultural references were very wide – he was an insatiable reader – and he seemed to have none of the notorious actors' foibles. I could not imagine him for a moment in the Hollywood actors' home, and then I could hardly imagine him either putting on grease-paint in a horrible mirrored dressing-room. His voice, his slow speech, his slightly glassy stare, his posture, the almost sinister affection he bestowed upon his rat – all were like nothing else in my experience, before or since, and combined with great sweetness, wonderful comicality and an extreme courtliness of manner to make me feel I had strayed into another time or society.

Hardly less mysterious seems to me the personality of Alec Guinness. On the couple of times I have met him (once in Holly-wood, once in Oxford) Guinness has treated me with a strangely rarified kindness, very different from his friend Richardson's eccentric joviality. He gives me the impression that in every action, every response, he knows exactly what he is doing. It is part of his genius that he never seems to be acting at all, on stage or off, but perhaps in fact he is permanently inhabiting a world of his own invention, and offering each one of us a role in it. His smile reminds me of the smile of the sculptured angel of Rheims, so inward and enigmatic is it, and he makes me feel that in all he does he is slightly amused – as though he is contemplating the part he is playing, the words he is saying, the stranger he is welcoming, the theatre and its pretensions, his art and even life itself with a cool sceptical affection. Nobody seems to exemplify more exactly the truth that all the world's a stage; and so perhaps Guinness enlarges the actor's perspective to make players of us all.

I have been lucky in my performers. I have admired most of them from a safe distance, I have met only good ones in the flesh, and have thus been spared the silly falsities, rivalries and affectations that are said to characterize their profession. Few of the actors and actresses I have encountered have been in the least actory, except in the noblest sense, and whether they have been towering figures of the world stage, or workaday supporting technicians, I have liked and respected almost every one of them. However, my ideal performer remains the same Douglas Fairbanks Jnr whom I met at lunch that day – not one of your strange virtuosi, like Richardson or Guinness, and certainly not one of those modest craftsmen whom I have imagined in their retirement, but the actor *in excelsis*, dashing, easy, marvellous to look at, full of charm.

I got to know him better later, and found him to be, as a star should be, as hospitable as he was cultivated. He could almost be an ambassador, the president of a bank, an admiral, a university chancellor, but never quite; for there is always to his presence, as I felt it in the restaurant, a confidential or familial projection of self. It is not merely that he expects you to recognize him, as my lesser actress in the bookshop hopes that you will recognize her. It is the knowledge that he has been for so many years part of your very life. He is like an ageless neighbour, or even somebody in the collective unconscious.

Straddling the actual and the imaginary, this sense of timeless acquaintance applies to all such universal stars, but I am particularly conscious of it in the presence of Douglas Fairbanks Jnr. Not only do I feel I have always known him, and remember his father too, Douglas Fairbanks Snr, dashing his own adventurous way through my childhood, but I rather think that long ago I had tea with his stepmother Mary Pickford, 'The World's Sweetheart', in the garden of her home Pickfair, 1143 Summit Drive, Beverly Hills, California, beneath bright awnings beside the swimming pool.

Or was that in a movie?

8
Jewish Friends

The first Jew I ever knew was a boy of my own age, a refugee from Vienna who came to live with us for a time shortly before the Second World War. He was the most brilliant person I had met. He spoke not a word of English when he arrived, but seemed to pick up the entire language in a month or two. He excelled at cricket, he played the violin exquisitely, Latin and mathematics seemed equally easy to him and to cap it all he was almost excessively good-looking. Though I was hampered by no false modesty myself, he made me feel gauche.

He left my life when he went away to school somewhere else, but I met him once again, on Reading station during the war. I had been newly commissioned, and was walking down the steps to the station subway, resplendent in Sam Browne and brand-new pips, when I saw him coming up the other way. He was a sergeant. We went together for a cup of tea at the buffet, and as I remember it our conversation was not constrained: but I knew, and he knew, that if either one of us should really be the officer, he should. It was because of his Jewishness, we both understood, that in theory (though mercifully not in practice) he ought to have saluted me when we parted.

I have never heard of him since – is he alive? Has he changed his name? Has he gone back to Austria? – and I expect he has long forgotten the incident. It left so powerful an impression on my own mind, however, that to this day I can remember the light and the smell of the station buffet, steam and clangings outside, Walter's graceful figure leaning against the counter, and the piquant feeling of bafflement and attraction that, then as now, I felt in the presence of Israel. 'Some of my best friends are Jewish' the old saying goes; as it happens, since my acquaintance with that dazzler from Vienna long ago, my life has been consistently linked with Jews, and all friendship apart I remain as profoundly fascinated and sometimes tantalized by the presence as I was on Reading station that day.

Like most of us I am held in spell by the allegorical nature of Jewry, to which we of the Christian culture have so long been educated. I myself regard the whole New Testament story as allegory, Jews from Judas to Jesus himself playing their essential roles in it, and allegorical too I find the State of Israel, that ultimate concentration of things Jewish which embraces within its borders, if only *de facto*, Calvary, the Dome of the Rock and Armageddon. I have known the State of Israel since before it was a State, and I have been conscious always of its condition as parable.

For a Gentile the chief pleasure of the Israeli republic in its formative years was to meet Jews of such spectacular confidence. It is true that years ago, arguing the Arab case with an Israeli girl in Jerusalem, I was horrified to find her bursting into tears of elemental sorrow – not political tears at all, but tears I thought of absolute inherited despair. Travelling with the Israeli Army, though, in the days when the Israeli cause seemed to almost all its participants a cause of self-evident and triumphant justice – travelling with those young men of Zion was an excitement of a unique historical kind. Never before, I suppose, has a people so long in exile, so frequently in bondage and so nearly annihilated, translated its genius so suddenly into a spirit of buoyant and intensely virile youthfulness.

It was like seeing a miracle, in miracle country. All the young Jews of the world, it seemed to me in 1956, were campaigning their way through Sinai: assembled from the ghettos and camps of Europe, fed upon fruit and honey, toughened in swimming-pools and clean deserts, tanned by sunshine, given a common language and inspired by an altogether new self-image. I had equivocal thoughts about the war they were fighting, but only affection for the soldiers and their style – when the battle was done the troops, dispersing from Sinai, mostly hitch-hiked their way home again, wearing a rag-bag assortment of semi-uniforms, and drinking vast quantities of the orange juice which was left here and there for anyone to use (courtesy, I seem to remember, of the canning company).

Allegorical in quite another way, and the most powerfully Jewish Jew I ever encountered, was Gideon Hausner, chief prosecutor at the trial of Adolf Eichmann in Jerusalem in 1961. It was Hausner's *job* to be allegorical, for the trial was a show trial, designed not merely to demonstrate the wickedness of the Nazis, certainly not just to punish the wretched Eichmann, but to rekindle in the Israelis their sense of immemorial Jewishness. The years have faded the details, but I see Hausner now at the front of the courtroom very black, black-haired, black-eyed, black-gowned, stooped, and as he talked he flapped his arms around a great deal, raising his hands to the sky, throwing them outwards, so that he looked like an ominous raven down there. His voice was deep and resonant, and he spoke in terrible hyperbole – about millions of lives and deaths, about thousands of years, about the emergence and destruction of nations, about prophets and martyrs and sacrifice and inexpressible evil. Nobody in the court, nobody in the world indeed, supposed for a moment that the accused would be acquitted, but Hausner was not really concerned with the day's justice, but with the whole unimaginable expanse of Jewish history. Pale inside his bullet-proof glass dock, wearing his headphones, the prisoner listened to him altogether impassively, as though he had heard it all before.

For myself, as I watched Eichmann hour after hour in his crystal cage, mild of manner but unquestionably the instrument of a million innocent deaths, I thought how much wiser the Israelis would have been to have handed him over to his own people, the Germans, to represent all our consciences – they were not all Jews who died in the concentration camps. But then perhaps the wisdom of the Jews, if it exists, is a wisdom specifically of the Diaspora, generated over the centuries by the fact of minority, the cruelty of exile, the absorption of all our cultures, and the fact, for example, that I was an officer, Walter an NCO.

Actually for many years I used to say that if I were a Jew I would certainly be a Zionist, and off with me to a kibbutz. I remember saying it to a Jewish colleague on *The Times*, a man of famous charm and literary distinction, and I can see his face now receiving my remark with a quizzical air of amusement – thinking to himself, I expect, how easy it was for a Gentile of easy enthusiasms to jump to such conclusions.

Today I am not so sure anyway, because just as I have come to surmise that Jewish wisdom may be by definition dispersed, so I find a kind of comfort in the presence of the Jews around the world. Even our market town at home in Wales has long been enlivened by the residence of a single Jewish family, which has provided not only characters of pungency and shopkeepers of skill, but also respected mayors. It is oddly reassuring to come across the little Jewish colony which has existed for 800 years at Cochin, on the steamy west coast of India, and moving to find a small synagogue riding the surfs of history in Hong Kong. I am happy to have been instrumental in arranging the marriage of a young Jewish glass-maker living in the first of all the ghettos, the ghetto of Venice; an American girl, reading an essay of mine about the place, was led to his atelier and fell in love with him – when they were married they invited me to a celebratory luncheon in New York.

As a matter of fact over the meal I took an extreme dislike to the bridegroom – Jews can be provoking, no doubt about it. My everyday associations with them, though, even with that glass-maker, have one and all been remarkable for a quality of enhancement. Something about them makes me live more lively, enjoy myself more – perhaps because they extend me mentally, there being an underlying sense of challenge in their company, or perhaps because my own attitude towards them is marked today, as was my attitude to my friend Walter all those years ago, by a sense of wonder. Most of the time of course I forget they are Jews at all, but when I have occasion to recollect the fact, and to remember by what astonishing routes of history they have come to be sitting beside me, once again they strike me as dramatically exotic acquaintances.

A Jewish friend of mine in Delhi, for instance, being a passionate horsewoman herself, established a kind of lien upon the social loyalties of a whole covey of equestrian maharajahs, polo-players to a man but as fascinated by the personality of their hostess as they were by her love of horses. They used to sit in her drawing-room, itself as I remember it a strange and wonderful melange of cultures, or sprawl on the lawn with long cool drinks, hanging upon her every word: dark moustachio'd military figures, handsome but rather running to plump, and in their midst my small vivacious friend, bestowing a chaff here, a compliment there, like a Jewish maharani herself.

And some of the happiest of all my evenings have been spent at the house of an old Jewish friend in Manhattan. He comes from a family of German Jews who, like so many others, long ago made themselves part of the New York Establishment, abandoning the rigidities of Orthodox Jewry and evolving into a mellow dynasty of Ivy League professional people. The guests, mostly Jewish themselves, are well-heeled, well-read doctors, lawyers, academics, journalists, charity workers, male and female, who have known each other for years, sometimes go on holiday together, meet at the Opera in an almost nineteenth-century way, and are affectionately familiar with all their host's foibles.

Which are many. He is particular about his food and wine and has a beguiling fondness for the oft-told tale. When he rises to his feet, as he often does towards the end of these convivial evenings, we all know that we are to be treated to some old favourites, delivered in a very slow, chuckling diction, interspersed with long drinking intervals and occasional bouts of a kind of anticipatory stammer. We none of us mind. He is so amused by the stories himself, his eyes shine so infectiously, we get such fun watching our fellow-guests pretending they do not know what is coming next, that all is as fresh and entertaining as ever.

I don't suppose these people often think of themselves specifically as Jews at all – they are, after all, quintessential New Yorkers, quintessential Americans too, and there is perhaps nothing especially Jewish to the nature of the evening. It is different for the outsider. Now and then, through the buzz and the laughter, I remind myself of the historical origins of the company, marvel once again at the threads of destiny that are brought together at that dinner-table, and feel a fanciful sense of achievement, even of home-coming, to be sitting there myself. In Wales we have always thought of ourselves as the Lost Tribe – why do you suppose so many Morrises, if they are not Welsh, are Jewish themselves?

9
Watching the Ships Go By

Whenever I can, wherever I am, I make for the waterfront to watch the ships go by. No pleasure is more reassuring. For one thing ships and boats are, at their best, among the most beautiful of all artefacts (I say at their best, because there are container ships sailing the seas today which are about as beautiful as dump trucks). For another thing they float, giving their movement a style at once soothing and exhilarating. And for a third thing, their transient presence on the world's horizons always seems to me like an assurance of companionship – one does not have to be stranded on a desert island to feel that if a ship is in sight all cannot be lost.

They remind me of the moon. Wherever you stand on the earth's surface it looks the same, and brings home to you with a poignant clout the brotherhood of all its watchers down below. Ships too seem utterly detached as they sail by, but link all humanity with their familiar shapes.

I came early to the watching of ships, because I grew up beside a Bristol Channel that was in those days one of Europe's great maritime thoroughfares. Only a grassy hill separated my home from the sea, and few anticipations have been more urgent for me than the climb up its flank, carrying my telescope, to see what vessels would reveal themselves for me on the other side – a plume of smoke first showing itself above the ridge, then a mast or two, or a funnel, until finally panting with exertion and expectancy I would throw myself on the grass, opening the slides of my telescope as I did so, to survey the morning's traffic.

I can see those ships now. There were handsome white banana boats making for Bristol, and freighters from West Africa, and

47

French wine ships, and ships piled high with timber flying the flags of Latvia and Lithuania, and fleets of blackened colliers coming and going perpetually from the coal ports of Glamorgan, and swift paddle-steamers taking holiday-makers to the piers of Penarth or Weston-super-Mare. Occasionally I would recognize, from the silhouettes in my *Dumpy Book of Ships*, some famous liner diverted from its usual route, a Canadian Pacific *Empress* or one of the new three-funnelled P&O's. This would give me the utmost excitement, besides adding to the interest of the otherwise somewhat monotonous journal in which I kept a register of these observations; and so ineradicable are the pleasures of childhood that to this day, when I see a ship at sea that I recognize by name, I feel an irrational surge of pride.

Only the other day, as it happened, I looked out of my window in Honolulu, Hawaii, and saw putting out to sea what I took to be an American battleship of the *Iowa* class. I called the public affairs office at Pearl Harbor to check, and great was my satisfaction to find that the ship was indeed USS *New Jersey*, 58,000 tons and almost half a century old. Ships are full of historical meaning, and none could be much more significant than this old leviathan. Thirty years ago few would have dreamed that such a warship, a full-blown battle-wagon, a dreadnought, would ever again put to sea. Battleships were a dead breed, so everyone thought, and in the age of the carrier and the submarine the last link had been broken with antiquity's ships-of-the-line. People wrote definitive books about battleships, confident that their tale was finished.

So to see that ship sail into the Pacific, retrieved from its mothballs after all, was an exciting moment for a ship-watcher like me – a dreadful moment too, for it is said that her guns now fire nuclear shells, and her very outline, all nine 16-inch guns ominously elevated, struck me as a terrible image of war's endlessness. Many dead ships around the world, permanently berthed or dry-docked at maritime museums, can give one an intellectual insight into the past; but never the thrill of living contact with history that a working ship can offer.

Even a gaudy cruise ship, which may seem at first sight a degradation of the whole maritime tradition, really stands four-square in the historical line. It perhaps looks silly, dolled up with bunting as it leaves the quay, its decks crowded with geriatric celebrants and supervised by Welcome Hostesses: but it is a great ship anyway, built by diligent shipwrights in a famous yard, powered by mighty engines, taken to sea now by its navigators on a voyage, very likely, far, far longer than any the liner captains of the past could contemplate.

I saw a Russian fish-factory ship sail out one day from the harbour of St John's, in Newfoundland, making for the Atlantic grounds where its trawlers were working. It hardly looked like a ship at all, so barnacled was it with electronic gear, so angular and ungainly was its shape. I waved none the less as it passed through the Narrows, and the slow long wave that responded from the wheelhouse seemed to me the very same wave that seamen have returned to watchers on that shore down all the centuries of the North Atlantic traffic – Basques and Bretons, Spanish and Portuguese fishermen, English merchant masters sailing to join their convoys, Canadian frigate captains and now, still constant to the trade, the Japanese and Russians in their peculiar craft.

Ship-watching is one of the basic pleasures of Venice. Although many of its old ship-kinds have disappeared within my own memory, even now for sheer variety nothing compares with the Venetians water-traffic – the deep-sea freighters, the barges, the water-buses, the speed-boats, the police launches, the fire-boats, the scavenger-boats, the yachts, the water-taxis and the immemorial gondolas. They are all around you. Looking up from a shop-window in the middle of town, suddenly you find the end of the street blocked by the huge white mass of one of those cruise-ships sailing by: a cameo of wondering passengers looking down at you from the rail, a shimmer of vapour from the funnel, a flutter of the stern-flag as it disappears behind the corner building, and then your alley opens out once more across the bright lagoon. Even better, gliding past a gap in the palaces you may see a passing gondola, and there is no class of vessel more irresistibly worth the watching.

The craft itself is beautiful, its lop-sided stance in the water is unique, the techniques of the gondolier are enthralling. Even the passengers repay observation, because a ride in the *sedia nobile*, the seat with its back to the oarsman, wonderfully elevates almost anyone's personality. I once observed a well-known film director sprawling in that seat, as his gondola proceeded down the Grand Canal, in a posture of magnificent grandiloquence, while on the seat facing him his assistant sat deferentially huddled. A little later, when I saw them again, they had changed places, and now miraculously it was the assistant who puffed at a cigar with every sign of self-satisfaction, while the great director opposite seemed to have been shrunken into obsequiousness.

My favourite Venetian observatory is the quayside below the Dogana, the old Customs House, which stands on an island promontory in the very heart of the inner lagoon. Here the vessels go by on either side, ceaselessly, large and small, and in a glittering panorama Venice displays itself around them. It is a scene of restless splendour. The tourist crowds jostle along the waterfronts, the flags fly, the small boats bob and race about, the gondolas toss stately in the swell, the noisy water-buses come and go; and loftily through the middle of the pageantry, as to the manner born, sail the big ships on their way to the docks – towering, but in a condescending way, above all those ancient roofs and islands.

I am not often moved by the ships of inland waterways, but the tow-boats of the Mississippi are exceptions – their voyages, after all, can be as long as Mediterranean passages, and their cargoes as heavy as any deep-sea freighter's. The best way of watching these ships, in my experience, is to eat a catfish meal at Natchez, Mississippi, which is the most entirely Mississippian town imaginable. Magnolia trees, southern belles, ante-bellum mansions, levées, memories of Southern epic, fantasies of Southern antecedent, the occasional Old Southern Steamboat (long since dieselized, actually), the Blue Cat Club, once described as 'the meanest, lowest-down, fightin' – and killin'est place in the world' – all these are Natchez, and so is the Natchez Landings Restaurant, whose nice old wooden building stands at the water's edge, whose porch has sensible wooden benches for lounging on and whose broiled catfish is the best in the western hemisphere.

Here is the place to go, preferably soon after dark on a warm summer evening, when if there is not in fact a heavy fragrance of cheroots and jasmine on the air, there certainly ought to be – here is the place to see a Mississippi ship go by. First of all, in point of fact, one hears it, in a distant boom or drum of engines. Then a searchlight appears far downstream, wavering across the water's surface, flickering here and there along the river banks. Finally out of the dusk emerges the immense Mississippi tow, from New Orleans bound for Cairo, for Memphis, perhaps for Pittsburgh a thousand miles up the Ohio – a string of steel barges long as an ocean liner, a mighty tug-boat at the stern: thrum-thrum of engines labouring against the flow, dim moving line of barges, and restlessly stroking the river bank, ever and again the long pale beam of the light.

At home I have only to walk to my window to watch the ships pass by: the slate ships of our sombre Welsh seas, loaded deep with the blue, green and grey stone of our mountains.

There they go, glorious three-masted schooners, proud as race-horses, with stout Welsh names like *Mary Jones* or *Prince Llewelyn*, and house pennants fluttering from their mainmasts. People call them the Western Ocean Yachts, so easy and graceful do they look. Sometimes I can recognize a master on his poop – Harry Hughes Porthmadog, perhaps, or Evan Roberts Borth-y-Gest. Sometimes I hear old Welsh songs across the water, and as the lovely vessels disappear from sight, sails billowing, foam streaming from the prow, I may whistle the music myself, alone at my window out of sight.

Out of sight, and you might say out of mind, for it is all illusion anyway. The slate trade died before I was born, and from one year to the next never an ocean-going ship really sails past my window. They are ships of dream, ships of yearning that I watch; but the sight of them is none the less liberating for that, for they represent in my imagination all the ships that ever sailed, past all our windows anywhere.

10

God, Kindness and Abyssinian Cats

It seems to me that the only honest religious attitude is agnosticism. We cannot possibly know the truth about God, creation and the after-life. There is a lie inherent to the deliberate belief in the unverifiable that religious people call faith, and casuistry to the suggestion that belief can be an act of will. Nevertheless I have myself been a pagan always, and more exactly a pantheist, preferring to suppose that the divine is not merely manifest in nature, but is actually nature itself. What else, after all, is the Christians' Holy Ghost? And is not the one unquestionable fact about the after-life the fact that our bones or ashes rejoin the natural cycle? This unsophisticated conviction was supernaturally confirmed to me one day after I had been listening, as I washed my hair in my Sunday morning bath, to a radio sermon. 'God is love' the preacher had declared, and I had countered him aloud through the shampoo. It should be the other way round, I told him. It's not that God is love, but that love is God – or rather, kindness is God, love being in my view too intense an abstraction to be universal (we can really hardly be expected to *love* our enemies, but we can certainly be kind to them).

Later that morning, as I walked down a lane on my daily exercise, I found myself debating that proposition too. How could I reconcile it with my own naturist beliefs? Nature certainly wasn't simply kindness – it was teeth, claw, decay, competition, blood, sex and hunger. But suddenly, truly as in revelation, I had an answer from nature itself. Suddenly every tree leant kindly towards me, every bush seemed to be smiling, and from the grass and the flowers beside the road, from the sheep over the stone wall and mountains beyond, I felt a glow of reassurance. Yes, they all seemed to be saying, kindness is the emotional figure of God, but the whole grand panoply of the natural order, fierce and placid, carnivorous or herbivore, crumbling into senility or awakening into new life, is the physical embodiment of kindness. Trust us! Keep walking!

I do trust them, and I believe that any cruelty and indignity practised upon the natural world, whether it be chemical farming or animal vivisection, is a direct affront to kindness and thus to the divine. And since this concept is necessarily woolly, like all religious conviction, I concentrate my thoughts about it upon the animals.

Long ago I came to realize that every single living creature, from a saint to a slug, from a rose to the most raggety weed, was of equal value in the eye of nature. We are all comrades, not waiting for some resurrected unity in the hereafter, but united now, and we should treat each other if not necessarily with affection, at least with respect. 'Why should I hurt thee?' said Sterne's Uncle Toby, releasing a fly through the window, 'this world is surely wide enough to hold both thee and me.' I am with him there. Flies are safe with me – mosquitos too, if they don't press their luck.

Nature is scarcely kindness in the Christian, turn-the-other-cheek sense. The tiger suffers not the little children, as she springs for the jugular of a baby antelope, and the whale gobbles up several million of its algal fellow-creatures, I am told, in every mouthful of sustenance. It is the heedless and unnecessary violation of natural laws that is evil: a man may eat a lamb with dignity, as a fox eats a mouse – may even give to the act some sacramental virtue if he thinks of it, between munches, as a symbolic affirmation of fellowship.

All this has made of me an animal liberationist of almost atavistic passion. A mild-mannered American episcopalian bishop, talking on Hong Kong radio one day about 'the sanctity of human life', found himself when he left the studio fallen upon by me with vituperative fury, so blind did the phrase declare him to be to the sanctity of life as a whole. In New York once I tried exclaiming loudly, whenever I saw a woman in the street wearing a mink or a Persian lamb, 'Oh, the poor animals', until I found that nobody took the slightest notice, assuming me to be merely another crazed bag-lady. I often emulate the character in one of Iris Murdoch's novels who, seeing a parrot caged in a pet shop, breathes the words

'I'm sorry' through the window: 'I'm so sorry, I'm truly sorry,' I say myself to captive creatures large and small, hoping they will understand me.

But if my obsession with animals has caused me anguish and bitterness, it has brought me infinite joy too, and this has been expressed above all in the companionship of Abyssinian cats.

It might have been goats, wittiest and most potent of the beasts, who have affected the course of empires in their time, and who are destined one day to take over the world in partnership with left-handed humans. It might have been donkeys: we had a couple for years, living wild on our brackeny hillside in South Wales, and I greatly respected their calm and kind intelligence. However I don't want the destiny of my own garden goat-governed too, and it is hard to establish intimacy with feral asses, so instead I have thrown in my lot with the cats. I remember as if it were yesterday the moment I set eyes on my first Abyssinian, bought for me as a present and sent to me in Wales by rail, all by himself in a basket. I met the train at Bangor station, and opening the lid of the basket, saw looking up at me with extreme confidence and cheerfulness what appeared to be a very small wild creature, ticked and gold-brown like a hare, with little tufts on the end of his ears. He gave me the impression that he had arranged the journey himself, having decided to emigrate out of a forest somewhere, and from that day to this I have regarded my Abyssinian cats as generous visitors from outer nature, kindly spending their lives with me.

Only the cat can give us this sensation. Dogs are disciplined, horses are enslaved, cows and pigs are exploited, goats are planning our subjection. Only cats join us as opportunistic partners. They do things for us, we do things for them, and when both sides feel like it we share the pleasure of each others' company. I find this arrangement exciting enough with any cat, even with the most homely of farmyard toms, descended from generations of cats next door; but with Abyssinians I find it thrilling, for they seem to bring into the house with them a suggestion of nature at its most defiantly untameable.

Not that the Abyssinian cat himself is in the least untamed. He is the most affectionate and easy-going of animals. But his form is so lithe, elegant and exotic, his manners are so sensuously graceful, and the look in his eye is sometimes so infinitely unfathomable, sometimes so mocking, that I can easily imagine him at night time, or when I am away from home, leading another life that is altogether his own. The cats of the ancient Egyptians, whom they mummified as sacred, were very like Abyssinians, and there are certain forest cats of Africa who appear to be close relatives.

The origin of the breed is in fact uncertain. I belong to a school – of course I do – which claims that the first examples came to Britain in the kitbags of soldiers returning from Lord Napier's punitive expedition to Ethiopia in 1868. There are some however who maintain that the Abyssinian originated in other parts of Africa, or in Asia, and even a few numbskulls who say it is descended merely from very refined and skilfully bred English tabbies. I made a special journey once to see the famous sacred cats of Axum, in northern Ethiopia, in the hope that I would find them to be obvious cousins of our Abyssinians. In those days they were officially maintained by the Cathedral of St Mary of Zion, on the grounds that their ancestors had been brought to Axum by the Virgin Mary herself, and each cat was supported by a particular patch of revenue-bearing land. There were six sacred cats when I was there, and I easily persuaded myself that their manner of mixed irony and bravado was very like that of the little creature in the basket on Bangor station; if I could not honestly claim they looked much like him, being a good deal plumper and more complacent, well, who would look lithe, thin and Pharaonic after a thousand years of episcopal bounty?

Whatever their roots, I like to think that my Abyssinians have given me an intimate link with the command post of nature, a chain of communication with headquarters. They have lived with me now through four cat generations, and though they have come to me with preposterous breeders' names, I have renamed them all after figures of Ethiopian myth or history: Theodore, Menelik, Solomon, Prester John – names of a wild grandeur, I like to think, by which I pay my own tribute to their other, private lives.

I am aware nevertheless that my cats are compromised. I do not entirely trust them, either – they may be spies, like dolphins, reporting to some unknown authority. When I want to experience the impartial immensity of nature I escape their surveillance and go down to the river in the evening. It is called the Dwyfor, and rising in the mountains seven or eight miles above my house, debouches into Cardigan Bay a couple of miles below. It is not very wide or deep, but it is very fast, and on a summer evening especially, for all the ravages of silage farming and air pollution, it is still full of life. I never see glow-worms nowadays, and toads seem rarer than they were, but there are still plenty of bats, and dragonflies, and sometimes a heron rises and flaps off ghost-like into the dusk.

There as darkness falls I sit on a rock to watch the water, and feel I am looking into the heart of all things. I know that when the night draws on the heroic sea-trout, making their way upstream to spawn in the mountain pools, will be swimming by me in urgent instinct, battling their way against rapid and waterfall, swift and bold and muscular: and thinking of them with admiration, though I cannot see them, I realize that nature's first message, the message of that Sunday morning revelation, is that the divine spirit is something strenuous and risky, comes in all kinds, and moves mysteriously.

11
The Travelling Craft

I have spent half my life travelling, and know that what they call the art of travel is really no more than a craft. There is nothing creative to it, nothing especially elevating, imaginative or even necessarily commendable. In my own case indeed it was long ago debased into a kind of addiction, reminding me of those video arcade machines which put you ashen-faced at the wheel of an imaginary racing car, hurtling around a conceptual track to the whirr of digital figures and the headlong approach of calamity. But a craft, yes. Travelling can be done well or badly, conscientiously or with a slovenly disregard of detail and nuance, and since for forty years it has been not only my compulsion, but also my profession and my abiding delight, I long ago drew up my own set of rules for its happy pursuance.

The first and most basic rule is this: that I can't see everything. I can't see anything *like* everything. I can't really take in even the few celebrated sights on the City Day Tour With English-Speaking Guides. The world is like a colossal art gallery, packed with treasures too rich, varied and marvellous for anyone to absorb in a dozen lifetimes, and even a single corner of it can only be explored selectively, as the wise gallery-goer decides to stick to Rembrandts one morning, Picassos the next. There are three pyramids to be inspected at Giza, but one is quite enough. There are Muslim, Hindu, Buddhist and Christian architectures to be observed in India, but no traveller can possibly pay intelligent attention to them all. Many frames of mind can sustain a journey – scholarly, sociological, gastronomic, carnal or just plain hedonist: but try to employ too many of them at the same time, and travelling becomes messy and unsatisfying.

Which brings me to my second self-precept: the need for a travelling theme. I never go without one. It matters not what the theme is. It could be the pursuit of some great historical or artistic progress, the spread of Islam, the development of the baroque in Colombia. It could be the spotting of engine-numbers in China or of great bitterns in the Norfolk Fens. It could be a deep-rooted interest in lying on sunny beaches drinking rum-and-Coca-Cola. Whatever it is, I stick to it. I let nobody persuade me to combine it, while I'm there, with excursions to onion-growing communes, or holiday courses in Galician folk-dance. I am there for the trains or the sun-tan! I spent ten full years journeying to a single theme, the rise and fall of Queen Victoria's Empire, and when I had exhausted it, until I found a new one my travelling went all to pieces; I missed connections all over the place and repeatedly forgot to collect the laundry.

Thirdly, I consciously expect my journeys to be enjoyable. I do not expect to be robbed, raped or poisoned, and generally I am not. When I *am* robbed or poisoned I pretend not to notice – there's always another day, I tell myself bravely, biting my lower lip and calling for rum-and-Coca-Cola. I never haggle; outrageous though the sum may sound, hissed at me by tout or cab-driver, I know that in a year's time I shall have forgotten about it anyway. I try never to grumble, even to myself, but simply remind myself, gritting my teeth, that things could easily be worse – I might after all be experiencing my own hypothetical epitome of an unhappy travel experience, namely to have been robbed of my passport and plane ticket, my luggage having already been lost in flight, while suffering from extreme diarrhoea during a high summer heat-wave and a severe water shortage, at a moment when the local electricity supplies and telephone services have been cut off because of political disturbances, with nothing to read but a Robert Ludlum thriller, expecting a visit from the security police in a hotel room without a wash-basin overlooking a railway freight yard on a national holiday in the Egyptian town of Zagazig.

My next precept is more debatable, because it concerns fundamental attitudes to the whole matter of travel. Some practitioners maintain that the essential purpose of moving around the world is to put yourself in other people's shoes, to experience life, as far as possible, as Frenchmen or Israelis or Japanese experience it, eating what they eat, buying what they buy, even trying to think as they do. Not me. Nothing is going to make a shogun of me, least of all ten days at a Yokohama motel, and scholars who have spent entire careers studying the Basque mind still can't make head nor tail of it. Far better in my opinion to regard the great world as a kind of show, a tragicomedy, kindly put on for my fascination. Nobody is offended by this approach. Most people love to be looked at.

And most people – my fifth rule of the craft – are agreeable, whatever their nationality. If somebody chances to pick my pocket or be rude to me on a bus, I try to bear in mind that it is not because he is German, or American, or Arab, or Indian, or English, but just because he is a thief or a yob like the ones we have in Wales. Sometimes this is difficult, I admit, and bigotry takes over despite myself. When two boys on a motor-bike once snatched my bag in Palermo, for an hour or two I damned all Sicilians, all Italians, all Latins, the Papacy, the Mafia and the entire Mediterranean culture: but I pulled myself together, and reminded myself that only two Sicilians out of five million had been in any way unpleasant to me – a proportion which, if extrapolated to cover the population of the world, would mean that there were no more than 2,000 bad-mannered persons on earth.

Such are my rules, and they work. I think of the pleasures of wandering as among the great joys of my life, while its miseries I recall only as the salt that gives them flavour. All the same, I sometimes suspect that the advantages of travel, however workmanlike, can be delusory. Occasionally I take time off to contemplate some small patch of my garden. It may only be a few feet square, a few inches even, but it is sure to be full of teeming life. Insects hasten about their business there, dewdrops hover, ferns creep cautiously from crannies in the stone, night and day alternate with the shadow of each passing cloud. All our own passions are being played out, I feel sure, microcosmically before my eyes. I recognize then that a narrowing of the vision can be as rewarding as a widening, and thus I read a last paradoxical principle of the travelling craft: that if it is fulfilment I'm after, I might just as well stay at home.

12
A Neighbour

When it comes to neighbours in my life, I think first and always
of Clough Williams-Ellis the architect, who lived along the coast
from me in North Wales. He was a frequent visitor to my house,
as I was to his, and I last saw him indeed on his death-bed, brought
downstairs to his comfortable work-room overlooking his garden.
He assured me then that he did not mind the thought of dying.
He had lived magnificently for ninety-four years, and if his spirit
was bright as ever his body was beginning to tire – a cataract one
year, a bad leg the next, told him it was time to move on.

The one thing that slightly worried him, he said puckishly,
was the thought of his own obituary in *The Times*, because those
anonymous records, generally written before their subjects' deaths,
could sometimes be unsympathetic and sometimes even malicious.
One never knew who might write them. So he had composed his
own, to be published in a posthumous book of memoirs, and he
showed me a proof of it: just like a *Times* example, in form as
in manner, but quite especially magnanimous about Sir Clough
Williams-Ellis, his work and his personality.

I was touched by this last expression of his vanity. However he
need not have been anxious about how the *The Times* would remember him, for it was I who had already written *its* obituary; and
since there was almost nobody who had given me more consistent
pleasure, entertainment, enlightenment and useful instruction, this
piece was almost as perceptive as his own.

Clough was a Welshman, one of the most distinguished of his time,
and he looked the part. Descended as he loved to claim from
ancient kings of Gwynedd, he bore himself with an aristocratic flair

that never quite crossed the line into mere eccentricity. Tall and beguilingly ugly (he had a face like an intensely amusing horse) he habitually stalked round his properties wearing a wide Spanish hat, knee-breeches, bow tie or stock, yellow waistcoat and bright yellow stockings. His feet, as I remember them, were rather splayed, his figure in later years became gracefully stooped, and even from a distance his movement, his gestures and indeed his very presence were altogether unmistakable. He was one of a kind, he would not have had it otherwise, and was careful to marry a wife, the former Amabel Strachey, who with her long skirts, dangling keys, formidable bearing and omniscient conversation was very nearly as individual as he was.

Clough was the less intellectual of the two, being I think emotional rather than cerebral as an architect, and empirical as a man. He claimed in that obituary of his to be 'however unfortunately, nine-tenths just his original self', but I suspect he owed some of his persona to the example of Frank Lloyd Wright, and some to Bertrand Russell, who became his neighbour and his tenant. Even in his aged eminence there was something innocent to him. His humour was frank and simple (great horse teeth flashing as he laughed), his taste in books was wide but often boyish (I remember Don Marquis and *The Wrong Box*), and he had a freely expressed preference for company that was witty, urbane, famous if possible or if not, rich – he was dazzled, I suspect, by the power to make money. If there was a side to him I did not like, it was a perceptible reluctance to suffer fools gladly; harmless and unimportant elderly persons were less likely to be subjected to his tremendous charm than dukes, Fellows of the Royal Society, bestselling novelists or Bertrand Russells. Children other than his own did not easily attract him, either – he was too busy of mind and attitude, too permanently engaged as it were, and preferred amenable little dogs who would not interrupt.

But children themselves liked the proximity of Clough (as they themselves, like all his friends, neighbours and colleagues, easily found themselves calling him). There was something particularly pleasant to his presence, something old but very clean, like a tree. Nothing was blurred or smeary about him. His colours were bright, his facial expressions were unclouded. He never slouched or shuffled and his most characteristic posture, at least in my own memory, was that of standing upright and intent at his drawing-board. For above and beyond all his flamboyance he was an artist, and when it came to architecture his mind was as erect as his physique.

Actually, as he never tired of telling people, he was not a qualified practitioner at all. The son of a scholarly and poetical clergyman, he simply set up shop on his own in the years before the First World War (during which he fought in France) and became well-known as an architect more or less of the Lutyens school. He built his first country house in 1912, his last in 1973, and they included what some critics consider the last great exemplar of the *genre*, Llangoed Castle in mid Wales. He also designed churches, hospitals, schools, clubs, a grave for Lloyd George, new premises for the Battersea Dogs' Home, a seaside café, a summit station for the Snowdon Mountain Railway, a couple of rectories and more than one model village. Yet he might be largely forgotten were it not, paradoxically, for his amateurism. He was a born amateur – an intuitive enthusiast of the eighteenth-century sort, whose vision was wider than mere fashion or technique. He was not a great architect, but he had a great gift for vistas, prospects, scenes, the ornamental and the picturesque. He was perhaps better at the spaces between the buildings than the buildings themselves, cherishing as he always did the overlap of art and nature.

All this led to the work which made him most celebrated, the pleasure-village of Portmeirion overlooking Tremadog Bay in Gwynedd, Wales. Portmeirion is just along the coast from my own home, and if I want to revivify my memories of Clough, all I have to do is go there. With all its faults and all its merits, it is himself perpetuated, and still to this day I can summon easily into fancy's vision, as I wander among its curious and festive structures, his yellow-stockinged figure coming up the hill, pointing out subtleties to visiting celebrities and basking in the recognition of passers-by.

Though Portmeirion may seem all frivolity, Clough built it with serious purpose – at heart he was a serious man. He wanted to demonstrate that even seaside commercial development, the most corrosive of all, need not clash with landscape or tradition, and to this end he built an architectural folly that could also be profitable. Acquiring a seashore mansion that had belonged, naturally, to a relative of his, together with a private headland tangled with rhododendron and azalea, he borrowed architectural motifs from the Mediterranean, acquired actual old buildings from here and there in Britain, added his own laughing touches of grace-note and allusion, and created a new kind of holiday resort. It was partly a hotel, partly a seashore park, and partly the fulcrum of a community of friends and sympathizers living either within the purlieus of Portmeirion, or in nearby houses and cottages.

Chiefly however, as Clough liked to say, Portmeirion was an exhibition of architectural good manners. For some tastes the manners are too contrived, and Clough, who tended to paint his lilies, added fancy to fancy so assiduously that in later years Portmeirion did come to seem a little overdone. But for me all was redeemed by the joy of the place, by its uninhibited delight in colour and humour, and by the lovely vistas of sea and distant mountain which, so meticulously exploited by its creator, gave Portmeirion its style. After all these years I seldom go there without finding surprises in its apparently guileless mixture, there on the sandy Welsh estuary, of the utterly incongruous and the perfectly proper.

Which was, of course, Clough's intention. It was not guileless at all, and Portmeirion remains his truest public memorial because it expresses with such cunningly applied gaiety his convictions about art, nature and synthesis.

Still, as a private declaration of his personality I prefer the garden which Clough made for himself at his own house, Plas Brondanw, a few miles inland from Portmeirion. It was here that I talked to him on his death-bed, and outside the window that day the garden seemed to lie in benevolent attendance upon him.

The Plas came into his possession when he was twenty-one, and over seven decades he cultivated its garden from desolation into perfection. It covers perhaps a couple of acres, much of it on sloping ground running away from the house; until the early nineteenth-century the wide valley of the Glaslyn below was an arm of the sea, and Clough used wryly to deplore the part his own ancestors had played in draining it for farmland. Even without the water, though, it is a glorious prospect. To the south is the shine of Porthmadog Bay, in the middle distance the river slides sinuously towards its estuary, in the north is the dramatic conical peak called Cnicht. All is dominated by the great bare mass of Yr Wyddfa, Snowdon to the English, the highest mountain in Wales and one of the most shapely in Europe.

This daunting and marvellous setting Clough determined to incorporate within his own demesne, bringing the glory of Yr Wyddfa itself into his own backyard. The task suited his genius well. He was not very interested in flowers, and his taste for the intricate was essentially a capricious delight in contrast – devices of decoration set against serene and patrician unities. To make the mountains part of his garden, his garden part of them, precisely exemplified his tastes, and for that matter his social values.

I love what he created there. I hate itsy-bitsy flower-beds myself, and loathe gardens conceived as botanical collections. Wandering in Clough's company around the gardens of Plas Brondanw always gave me a pleasure that was almost an excitement, so absolutely was this place the achievement of one man's lifetime. He had arranged it as a kind of belvedere over the river valley. A fine old ilex stood in the middle of it all, shading the lawn, and there were box hedges and dark clipped yews around ('While you sleep,' Clough used to quote a gardener of his youth, 'they'll be growing . . .') Here and there were characteristic fancies – a memorial to a beloved terrier, sculpted worthies and divinities, the royal cipher which did not in the event go up on a village post office he designed. 'Just look at those damp stains,' Clough would say with mock-dismay when we reached the garden pavilion: he had introduced them artificially as he built it.

At first sight it might seem an easy-going garden in the Anglo-Italian kind, but actually it was slyly and even arcanely arranged. Clough was all Celt, and his setting of his garden against its background was a little reminiscent of ley lines, cromlechs or standing stones. There were calculated sight-lines everywhere, and Clough loved displaying these ingenuities, carefully following a set course around the garden so that each device would fall into place in proper order and at the proper time. The climax came when you reached the south-west corner of the garden, and like a magician, however many times you had done the tour before, Clough bade you turn around to look up the narrow vista to the other end. There you found, framed stunningly between the trees, the spectacular pyramid of Cnicht, which I used dutifully to pretend I had never noticed until that moment, and which indeed stood there fierce and sudden against the sky just as though Clough had put it there himself.

It was right that he should die at Plas Brondanw, rather than at Portmeirion; a slight hint of the melancholy always seemed to me to give an extra meaning to the house, and this, I think, was part of his personality too. He was ebullient to a degree, inexhaustible in fun and energy, and in the last years of his life declared himself to be 'that rare animal, a truly happy man'. Nevertheless I often detected in him a strain of sadness. It may have come from his ineradicable memories of the First World War, or from the death in action of his only son in the Second. It may have been the subconscious instinct, familiar in such obvious winners, that life's prizes were less than satisfying after all.

He was a lifelong agnostic. When he died indeed, and a suitably squirely memorial was carved for erection in the local village church, the parishioners declined to accept it, just as there were bureaucratic objections to his wish that his ashes should be shot by rocket into the sky. On the whole he tended to the belief that our one life on earth was all we had. When he was in his early nineties, however, he told me one day that he was having second thoughts about the possibility of an after-life – a wistful reappraisal not uncommon, I imagine, as the day of truth approaches. I proposed that if this hunch proved correct he send me a simple message from the beyond. From time to time he used to consult my 29-volumed *Dictionary of National Biography*, and I suggested that if ever he needed to consult it after his death – it might be convenient, I thought, for checking the credentials of his fellow-departed – he deliberately replace its volumes in the wrong alphabetical order.

It is ten years since he died, and whenever I go home to my library I look to see if Clough has used the *DNB*. So far he never has. Perhaps there is another set available to him, or perhaps he was right in the first place.

13
American Joys

If the hitch-hikers are American I usually stop for them. One can generally tell. They try harder for their lifts, holding up well-lettered destination signs and offering ingratiating smiles. Not for them the mechanical jerk of the thumb while looking the other way; they are in the lift-getting business, part of the business of travelling in Europe, and they do the job properly.

When they are on board they generally work for their keep, too. They do not sit there slumped and morose, like so many travellers of other nationalities. They tell me all about themselves, they learn all about me, they may give me a brief lecture upon the social customs of my own country, or kindly correct me when I appear to be going the wrong way. They are generally willing to oblige. 'Are you going to Scotland?' one young man asked me when I stopped for him just outside London. 'No, I'm going to Wales.' 'OK, make it Wales' – and I drove him all the way to Bala, and left him smoothly chatting up the farmer's wife at a bed-and-breakfast place.

In many ways these people epitomize the pleasures America has given me through life. I am not entirely deceived by them. I know their charm is partly delusive, and that sometimes, if I decide against picking one up, he makes a rude gesture at me from behind. I am not invariably amused when told by somebody from southern California that I am mispronouncing the name of Cirencester, and I occasionally feel that I have been unjustly chosen for a back-seat re-run of a summer school course in medieval art.

But I greatly enjoy the buoyancy of them, amounting in the best instances to what American Jews call *chutzpah*. 'If you don't wanta get on, bud,' said a slogan popular in the United States when I was young, 'move over, and make way for a guy who does.' Not very elevating sentiments, but undeniably forceful, and sometimes inspiriting too. I have never, on the whole, wished I had been born an American; but I would think my life deprived of a happy dimension if I had not spent so much of it on the other side of the Atlantic.

Like many another of my generation, I had dreamed of the place always. I dreamed of it romantically because where I grew up, on the Bristol Channel, the fact that no land stood between us and New York afforded me, at sunset especially, tantalizing visions of Manhattan's towers and palaces. I dreamed of it in an entertained way, like everyone else, at the cinema – even in the 1930s, when I imagine not one in ten thousand inhabitants of the British Isles had ever crossed the Atlantic, we were all strangely familiar with American scenes and idioms. Finally, when I was much older, I began to dream of it actually in my sleep. I dreamed repeatedly of a particular kind of office door, opening upon a street: not at all a modern or glitzy door, but surprisingly homely, perhaps the door of some old-fashioned family establishment, with varnished wood, and lots of brass about. Outside this door the street life of America, as I saw it in my sleep, proceeded with none of the Hollywood flash, but solidly and respectably.

All these dreams, the waking ones and the sleeping ones, were presently to be fulfilled. The entertainment was confirmed first. Before joining the army in the Second World War I worked for a few months, as a very young reporter indeed, on a newspaper in Bristol, where many ships from the North Atlantic convoys made their landfalls. I was sent one night to report on a performance of Irving Berlin's US Army troop show *This Is The Army*, which had just arrived in Europe to bolster Allied morale (Berlin appeared in it himself, singing a very frail tenor, which I can still hear, a song he had written in the *first* World War entitled 'Oh! How I Hate To Get Up In The Morning').

As representative of the *Western Daily Press*, though only in my seventeenth year, I sat in the very front row of the Victoria Assembly Rooms, not far from His Worship the Lord Mayor.The soldier musicians of the band, only a few feet away from me in the orchestra pit, were amused by my callow presence there, and threw

68

cheerful surmises at each other, loud enough for me to hear. 'Won a raffle ticket.' 'Bribed the usher.' 'Murdered the guard.' 'Blackmailed the mayor.' Eventually one of the brass players turned to me directly. 'C'mon kid,' he said, 'come clean. You *know some-body*, doncha?' – and in that very moment, as they looked laughing across at me, I was captured by the particular American mixture of quick wits, frankness, arrogance and good nature that has beguiled me ever since.

My childish vision of bright lights and soaring towers came true for me, as it comes true for nearly everyone, the moment I set foot for the first time in New York. I had sailed there on the liner *Mauretania* (the second and uglier of that name, once likened for me by a Cunard official to a woman whose eyes are too close together) and was met at the dock pier by a functionary from the Harkness Foundation, which had given me a fellowship. This sensible fellow took me at once by cab to Times Square, up through the shining skyscrapers, across the dizzy streets, to the pageant of lights, unique in those days, that was Broadway. Next day he put me on the Twentieth Century Limited, perhaps the most beautiful railway train ever built, and I went on to Chicago cherishing images of Manhattan at least as marvellous as the ones I had first fancied from the other side of the ocean.

As for my third dream, the sleeping dream, that was to be fulfilled more slowly, and less obviously. That office door, I later came to realize, is very common in America. I saw it often as soon as I arrived, and I see it often still. I have come to interpret it as representing something quite different about America, which has grown upon me over the years – something unexpectedly *venerable*. The United States is no longer a young country. It has the oldest of all written constitutions, and in many ways it is devoted to precedent, style and tradition. Circumstances introduced me very early to this aspect of American life, in the persons of academics, mountaineers, newspapermen of a certain kind and a variety of author, and I have always reminded myself of its values, as I might hang on to that polished brass doorknob, when from time to time the general awfulness of things American has threatened to repel me.

Thus I have myself interpreted the dream of the door, but others have carried it further. An old colleague of mine in New York says it is an allegory of sincerity. He believes that American sincerity works in different ways from its European equivalent. On the surface, he maintains, your average American is friendlier than your European; one layer down, the European is truer than the American; but to the American sensibility there is another, extra layer, summoned from all the inherited mass of suffering, exploitation, enterprise and sacrifice which is the national experience. This deepest trustworthiness, he maintains, gives Americans a stauncher loyalty and a profounder capacity for friendship.

I fear if it was ever true in the general, it is fading every year, as America's historical instincts shift. I have found it, however, perfectly true in the particular. Acquaintances I have thought speciously charming have turned out to be, at moments of distress or awkwardness, true as gold. Transient Europeans, even those most congenitally suspicious of America, invariably admire the courtesy of the people, but having myself been through troubled times in the United States, I know it as something stronger. My New Yorker may be right. It is the strength of that mahogany door, and the integrity of the once deep-etched lettering on the brass nameplate, now worn thin by generations of careful polishing.

My first stay in America coincided with the Senator McCarthy business, when that unlovely politician, abetted by his young lawyer cronies Roy Cohn and David Schine, stalked the land ruining reputations and demeaning the Constitution with false accusation. New as I was to the scene, I was dismayed by this spectacle. Not only was McCarthy plainly a vicious and probably dishonest demagogue, he was also depressingly unattractive, while his assistants looked to me like no more than a couple of card sharpers. The whole performance, televised day after day in bars and hotel lounges wherever I went, seemed like something out of Nazi Germany – the same mean cruelty, the same ugly faces, the same poor baffled victims and alas, so far as I could see, much the same public apathy. Sometimes the whole country seemed ripe for despotism.

I had an introduction to Felix Frankfurter, at the time the most famous judge of the Supreme Court, and I expressed these feelings to him. He dismissed them. The worst would never happen, he said. The United States was a pendulum, a nation of compromise held in balance as much by instinct as by constitution, swinging now to one extreme, now to another. The centre would always hold. It was embodied in the law and in the tradition, his own court was its guarantor, and sooner or later the pendulum would return there. In the case of McCarthy he was right, and I remember with delight the spectacle of the lawyer Joseph Welch, a genial attorney of the old school, finally in one of the classic television confrontations cutting the evil senator down to size – 'I weep for you, Senator, I weep for you . . .' I have often had my doubts about Frankfurter's thesis in wider application, but it is true that the equilibrium has sustained itself. Warlike and peaceable by turns, liberal and conservative, grand and ridiculous, violent and conciliatory, admirable and shabby, so far in its wobbly way the United States has stuck to its historic course as the country above all others where a man has a statutory right to the pursuit of happiness – the key proposal, in my view, of the Declaration of Independence, articulated very properly by a Welsh-descended revolutionary, Thomas Jefferson.

Of course one can pursue happiness corruptly or maliciously, but perhaps that is the price the nation pays for its Jeffersonian liberties; if men were always virtuous, as Madison once said, there would be no need for government at all. I have to admit that for me part of the pleasure of America has been its never-ending and pyrotechnical display of every human emotion, bad or good. With a shameless anticipation I pick up my newspaper, every day in America, expecting – hoping? – to find some astonishing new scandal, disgrace, revelation, allegation or public absurdity. Despicable though I find the American tendency to spit upon their fallen idols, still I watch the spectacle almost as eagerly as I watched Welch (who went on, by the way, to become a film star in his old age) humiliating McCarthy that day. Politicians making fools of themselves, lofty women stripped of virtue, sanctimonious clerics revealed in compromising situations – I hate to say it, but in America they really do add to the national exuberance, and all too often to the national merriment.

Liberty, I suppose, brings out the worst as well as the best in us, just as America, so the poet Philip Bailey wrote, has 'something good and bad of every land'.

71

I wrote a book about the United States, after my first year there. I was twenty-seven years old, and knew everything there was to know. One of my prophecies was that before too long a homogeneous mediocrity would overcome the Americans, issuing from what people then called Middle America, and later the Silent Majority. I had spent my fellowship searching out minorities and anomalies across the country, from New England Shakers to Montana shepherds, and had reached the conclusion that they would not last much longer – all would be swallowed up in uniformity.

I was quite wrong. I didn't know everything after all, and except in superficials the style of the country seems to me as varied as ever. There used to be some visionaries who envisaged a United States broken up into nine or ten separate republics, and I can easily imagine it still – a republic of New England, republics of the east and of the north-west, a prairie republic, Hispanic California, Texas of course, the Old South and the city of New York a sovereign entity of its own. Once again the pendulum effect has worked. Since I wrote my book America has passed through half a dozen immense social, ethnic and even moral convulsions, and each one of them has helped to ensure that the nation has never congealed into any boring sameness. We have had the McCarthyites and the liberals, the hippie and the flower people, space travel and Kennedy and Nixon and Carter and Reagan and Viet Nam. We have had LSD, AIDS, Watergate, the Moral Majority, Women's Lib. We have had amazing racial changes: first the fateful emancipation of the blacks, then the still more far-reaching proliferation of Asians and Hispanics, which is fast changing huge areas of the country into altogether other kinds of society.

Some of these progressions have been terrible, of course. The twin advance of violence and the drug culture has made many Americans as fearful for their lives today as their European forebears were in the Middle Ages – a Jewish ghetto in sixteenth-century Poland was probably safer than a slum in late twentieth-century America. I could hardly have conceived, when I morosely forecast America's dulled homogenization, that in some of the very towns which so depressed me with their conventionality in 1954, women would be afraid to walk the streets in 1989.

Still, draw what morals you may, all these various spasms, tendencies and reactions have helped to keep America inexhaustibly varied and interesting. It is a much more interesting country now, in fact, than it was when I first saw it, inhabited by a wider spectrum of humanity and dominated by more various aspirations. Its exceptions have not been ironed out, its excesses wax and wane still. It is hard to be bored in America, unless I suppose you run a middle-sized turkey farm in the outskirts of Indianapolis.

It is partly because it sounds interesting that America's immigrants go there, and if ever I retire I would rather like to go to a secure and efficiently door-manned apartment somewhere in mid-Manhattan, where the unending interest of things, spiced perceptibly with danger, would keep me young and on my toes. As it is, whenever I go to the United States (which I have done annually without a break for thirty-five years), I find myself if not actually rejuvenated, at least re-animated. Years ago I came first to distrust, then to detest America's role in world affairs, and I still wish the Republic would withdraw once more into its own isolation and leave us all in peace. But private America delights me as ever, and many of my happiest memories are memories of its ebullience and its style.

I remember a tumultuous rainy night, for instance, when there was a pop concert in aid of charity in New York's Central Park. The heavens opened that night, the park was turned to mud, the streets flowed with water, but the hundreds of thousands of young people at the concert made a jamboree of it. People sloshed merrily here and there in gumboots, sprayed each other by riding bicycles through puddles, hilariously raised tattered umbrellas to the wind and surged about the flooded sidewalks on roller-skates. The very policemen, buttoned to their noses in streaming waterproofs, found it all highly comical, and I myself staggered back to my apartment, soaked to the skin from head to foot, in such a state of exuberance that you might have thought it had been raining champagne.

Then only the other day, taking the night train from Chicago to New York, I felt myself all but overcome by the sheer human grandeur of the United States. After dinner in the restaurant car I walked back through the darkened coaches to my sleeper, as the great train laboured across the continent towards Cleveland, Toledo, Buffalo and Albany, over many a gleaming river and through many a slumbering hamlet. Lurching and swaying I made my way back, coach after coach, and as I went I saw to right and left of me, exposed in the innocence of sleep, the faces of young America. They were black, and brown, and white, and yellow, some more handsome than others, some scrunched up against seat backs, some thrown back with open mouths; but seen as a whole that night, as we plodded on across the continent, they moved me with a most poignant sense of beauty – the beauty of the American idea, really. Few of those travellers were old, none of them were rich, or they would not be travelling coach class on Amtrak; some lay in each others' arms and one had a pet turtle sleeping too upon his chest; sentimentalist that I am, it brought tears to my eyes to see them.

I have met some very odd Americans. The British are proud of thinking themselves eccentric, but I suspect the proportion of odd-balls is much higher in the United States. Moreover they are more readily accepted, and most of the powerful Americans I have met have been true originals, having gained their power because of their originality. Sometimes this makes for unlikely memories. I recall Harry Truman, for instance, rising from his desk in an unpretentious office block in a commercial street of Kansas City, hitching his trousers up, walking jauntily across the room and twirling a globe for all the world as though he wanted to sell it to me, cut price; actually he was demonstrating not simply the lie of the Iron Curtain, but his personal sealing of it as President, in effect, of half the world. I remember with astonishment still an evening I spent at the Manhattan home of David Rockefeller, one of the world's greatest financiers: I had never met him before, and he had never heard of me, but I had popped a letter through his front door expressing the desire to see how an American millionaire lived, and he had invited me over for an evening with his family – his wife liked my handwriting, he said. Austin Tobin, chairman of the Port of New York Authority and thus one of the most powerful public servants in America, was a high romantic of Tennysonian sensibility: he told me once that during the Second World War, when from his office window he used to see the camouflaged *Queen Mary* sailing out alone to face the terrible hazards of the North Atlantic, he would cry out loud 'Go it, old girl!' I first met Jann

Wenner, the founder of *Rolling Stone* magazine and to my mind a journalistic genius, when he was still in his twenties: we dined together at a restaurant in San Francisco, and when I happened to admire the rattan chairs of the place he instantly asked the waiter to have a couple sent to me in Wales.

But then surprise and paradox are American essentials. I sometimes wonder how the nation ever regenerates itself, so utterly unmaternal do most young American women seem, and how a populace which represents itself as being almost universally disturbed can achieve such hard-headed things. I marvel in particular at the contrast between the sharpness of American thought and the verbosity of American expression. In this country, Saul Bellow says somewhere, mere words carry little meaning, and it can be true. 'Everything OK?' asks the maître d'. 'Just terrible,' one replies. 'Fine, fine,' he says, and continues his rounds complacently.

The interest of America is re-created generation after generation. In particular the matter of the Indians, the only original Americans, recurs throughout the national story in different moods or tones of voice. Even in my own lifetime the Indian place in national affairs has been transformed. When I first went to the United States I declared them, in that grand mis-prophecy of mine, doomed to impotent absorption in the whole; thirty-five years on they are winning sophisticated law-suits all over the place and regaining enormous slabs of the national resource.

I hope that is not the reason, but my own responses to the American Indians have been similarly revised. I used to think them, by and large, very tedious. As I wandered their reserves I often felt that I never wanted to see another bead necklace, another corn dance, another reconstructed Sioux encampment for as long as I lived. I was sceptical about the alleged profundity of the Indian cultures, and I despised the way in which the tribes appeared to have sold out to the tourist trade. They seemed in many ways an object lesson to my own people, the Welsh, whose predicament of identity is much the same.

But I have changed my views, and though I will still happily forego another visit to the bead museum I have come to admire the secretive tenacity of these peoples, and to respect their cultures after all. Perhaps we have all learnt to wish, as we have come to know the alternatives, that we too could be as close to the earth and the animals, the stars and the moon. For me this reappraisal reached a fulfilment a few years ago when I spent Christmas morning at the Pueblo Indian village of Santo Domingo, in the bare brown country south of Santa Fe. Even then I expected the worst of the function widely advertised as taking place that morning – Santo Domingo is just off a main road, and I assumed the goings-on would chiefly be aimed at the passing holiday traffic.

I was wrong again. Only a handful of gringos were there, and the protracted rituals were performed with an exhibitionism that was, I thought, entirely introspective – half Christian, half pagan, and comprehensible only to the Pueblo Indians themselves. The dancing and the drumming, the chanting and the swaying, the parade line after line of splendidly costumed men, women and children, struck a plangent chord in my imagination. Many of the dancers, I knew, worked in shops and offices in the town, and all of them watched TV, drove around in pick-ups, ate hamburgers in fast food stores and sold their not very covetable crafts at souvenir stands. Yet there they were honouring with a cheerful power and enthusiasm the confused beliefs of their ancestors, evolved on that very same ground before the American Republic was born. They were not the roaming, scalping Indian kind; they were village Indians, settled in the same place for centuries, and through all the kaleidoscopic shifts of American history, all the comings and goings of the great men and charlatans, all those daily newspaper sensations, all the wars and ups and downs of economic fortune, they had remained in their hearts the same.

It seems a good moment, as they prance by me now with drumbeat, bells and quivering feathers, to conclude an essay about American joys.

14
On Success

Of all the sentences I have written in the course of a literary life, only two have regularly been quoted back at me. One is the last line of a book on Venice – 'No wonder George Eliot's husband fell into the Grand Canal.' The other I wrote, parodying Milton, in an earlier book of memoirs: 'Shame is the spur.'

The first sentence was omitted from the German translation of the book, on grounds, I assume of frivolity. The second, no more than a casual fancy, has been interpreted by most of my respondents as an admission of a guilt complex, which the *Encyclopaedia Britannica* defines as a 'subjective awareness of having violated personal, familial, religious or societal norms, the offence being real or imaginary'. In fact I meant something quite different. I meant that when in life I have succeeded in something, it is generally because I have been ashamed to fail. The impulse however is hardly less neurotic than those feelings of self-reproach so dear to the psychiatrists. One can of course be genuinely and properly ashamed of oneself, but far more often one is ashamed of what other people will think, and conversely I suspect that more often than not the pleasure of success is nothing more admirable than the pleasure of showing off.

Having performed disgracefully few altruisms in my life, I cannot say if the pride of having helped others can be a genuine, humble, inner pride – not often, I suspect, most saints seeming to prefer recognition of their saintliness. And never having done anything very terrible, either, I don't know how often criminals are satisfied with crime entirely unnoticed. I can only admit that in my experience the satisfaction of literary achievement, fitful though it be, is chiefly the dual gratification of gaining admiration and avoiding humiliation. I know very well what a bubble reputation is – I know

77

all about being true to oneself – I know that success and failure are imposters both – but somehow good sense and proper standards are instantly lost, when a newly-published author buys the paper on Sunday morning, and turns anxiously to the book pages.

Yet as those poets told us (and Kipling at least should know, having himself run the gamut of critical adulation and contempt) it is a lot of nonsense. Lord Castlereagh the Foreign Secretary actually preferred unpopularity – 'more convenient and gentleman-like', he thought. A fulsome request for an autograph one day, a sneer behind the hand another, they count no more than a gleam of sun or the shadow of a cloud. What does it matter? Who cares? I have all my own books expensively bound in leather, stack them in a revolving bookcase and from time to time show them to visitors, but logic tells me that nobody else in the whole wide world is much interested in the collection. When I die one or another of my children, I suppose, may mildly cherish the volumes as keepsakes, but nobody will really look at them, let alone read them, ever again.

All is vanity! But I am not denying of course the pleasure of success, or even denying it some merit. The first public success I achieved (and I have never had another like it) was my one and only newspaper scoop, on Everest in 1953, when my dispatch from the mountain to *The Times* not only broke the news of the first ascent providentially on the day of Queen Elizabeth II's coronation, but simultaneously made me, as Andy Warhol was to put it later, famous for fifteen minutes. The moment when, turning on the radio in my tent somewhere in the Sola Khumbu country, I learnt that my message had reached London safely, was a moment that changed my life. The world seemed to open its doors for me. Dinners and banquets beckoned me. I was interviewed in other newspapers, writing engagements multiplied, my first book was commissioned and in a flash I was awarded a fellowship in the United States. I seemed to float on a nimbus of success. Anything seemed possible.

My ego walked on a knife-edge – I may actually have become insufferable, I may just have escaped. However the longer effects of this somewhat precocious success were, I am sure, only beneficial. Professionally it did me nothing but good, and psychologically too

I believe it to have been a wholesome shot in the arm. On the one hand it made me think, at least for a few years, that there was nothing I could not do; on the other hand it gave me an early inkling of life's tinsel. Through my self-satisfaction I did dimly recognize how ill-considered public esteem could be, and how ridiculous its values. Yet the very fact of success somehow eased the challenge of life, relaxed my ambitions and perhaps made me a better person after all. To this day I feel those conflicting responses within me whenever (as still often happens) ageing strangers recall the thrill of the news from Everest nearly forty years ago, and butter me up with compliments.

Since then I find I have experienced some kind of public exposure about every five years – another fifteen minutes of fame. This has not been arranged to plan, and indeed the quarter-hour of renewed visibility has sometimes been extremely unwelcome. The original revelation of my trans-sexualism, while it certainly set my adrenalin running, first wounded me terribly and later bored me to distraction. Occasional forays into politics (Welsh nationalist, anti-monarchist, animal liberationist) have left me severely shaken by vitriolic responses. Being short-listed for the Booker Prize, in 1986, which seemed to me on the face of it an altogether desirable event, turned out to have a backlash, so particularly virulent were the opinions of those who did not think my book a suitable choice – opinions which, ironically enough, I shared. However I have enjoyed two or three moments of less equivocal literary success, and I had a period of television display in the United States, when people would powerfully bolster my self-esteem by recognizing me in the street or asking me to sign books in restaurants. Either way, the successive brief moments of public attention have simultaneously strengthened my confidence and my scepticism, confirming my view that success, while it is certainly not all good, is not all bad either.

In moderation, that is. Though some extremely famous people I have come across seem able absolutely to defy the corrosion of celebrity, in many more its depredations are obvious, and even the strongest are vulnerable. I was told once about the momentary chagrin of the then best-known television personality in Britain when a bell-boy in Leeds, approaching him, his director and cameraman in a hotel lobby, inquired innocently which of the three was Mr Richard Dimbleby. The pleasure of being recognized, which I have experienced in the most minor degree, must be very corrupting to those permanently experiencing it, besides being extremely exhausting; and it is this visual fame, in particular, which gives to the true celebrity that queer veneer of unreality, like a glowing mask, which is most apparent of all in the aspects of soap-opera stars and minor British royalty.

Even at my level, success tarnishes. I am foolishly disappointed if, having paid in a bookshop with a credit card, I find the assistant does not recognize my name. When strangers, discovering my profession, ask me who I am, I generally decline to tell them – not out of modesty, but because of the rebuff I feel when (as almost always happens) they have never heard of me. Oh, the petty pride of it! I have never cared about being rich, I do not covet power, but Milton's original apothegm applies all too exactly to me: when it comes to success, fame more than achievement is truly the spur – I am ashamed to admit.

15
My Favourite City

After half a lifetime of urban wandering I had been asked so often to describe my favourite city that in the end I made one up. This was not as easy as it sounds, because the cities I like best are not generally the nicest ones, or the most comfortable, or the loveliest. I wanted no Viennese *gemütlichkeit* to my ideal municipality. I wanted nothing as architecturally perfect as Venice, as terrific as Hong Kong or New York, as optimistically buoyant as Sydney, as grand as Paris, as assured as London. I required a touch of pathos to the place, an element of perennial confusion and a hint of shady dealing. In short, I resolved for a start that the place must embody the pungent mixture of vices and virtues that we call Levantine.

But where in the Levant should it be? Certainly not in the ever-warring Middle East, and preferably indeed not within the frontiers of any existing State. My city must stand, I determined, somewhere beyond the perimeters of contemporary affairs; so I invented a peninsula for it, and made it an independent City State, and called it Hav.

I grew exceedingly fond of the place, and the characteristics it developed in my mind were those that, in my opinion, the best real cities ought to have. It was beautiful, within reason – a sea-city of the nearer east, offering its aficionados all that the status conventionally implies in the way of the heroic and the picturesque. At the same time it was sufficiently remote to escape the dead hand of tourism. It possessed no deep-water harbour for cruise ships, it was too bumpy and poor for an airport, and it was separated from its Turkish hinterland by an abrupt and cave-riddled escarpment.

Only a single railway line entered it, together with a precipitous unpaved road. This isolation not only kept out the package tours, but also gave the peninsula a bottled effect, preserving its indigenous sense of slightly flattened fizz. Town planners had never been let loose upon it, so that it was free of pedestrian precincts, malls or unnecessary spaces, and international conservationists had never heard of it, so that its buildings were left to age in a true and becoming crumble.

Then Hav was cosmopolitan without being assimilative. It was no melting-pot. In my ideal city separate communities of race or religion kept their identities intact, their petty prides and rivalries giving spice to the urban life. Hav was wonderfully rich in minority enclaves, none of them being either dominant or downtrodden, and was ornamented everywhere with the steeples, minarets, domes, pagodas and miscellaneous towers of a dozen faiths and architectures, each one more assertive than the next.

Life in such a city must be, while never placid or uneventful, endemically leisurely. If there were emergencies, they must be slow subtle ones, and all the workings of the town must be, while tinged with the procrastinations and lesser fiddles essential to the Levantine condition, nevertheless easy-going and humane. I wanted no stony incorruptibles running my favourite city. Give me a fallible rascal any day, and let me zlip a zloty, a dinar, a rouble or a Hav kuru into the back of his hand.

And of course Hav required a history. A city's history need not, in my view, be long to be satisfactory, but it should be complicated. Hav's turned out to be labyrinthine. Even I could not always remember the tumultuous sequence of events in the peninsula, where empires had succeeded empires down the ages, where Arabs had confronted Celts. Slavs had mingled with Mongols and the Silk Route had brought its camel caravans out of China. Specious treaties had been signed there, meaningless alliances had been concluded, political subterfuges of every kind secretly consummated. In short the tide of human affairs had sent ripples beyond number to lap the peninsula, and sometimes indeed to flood the great waterfront square, the centre of all things in Hav, which lay between the gates of the Arab quarter and the Russian-built railway station.

All this was my fancy, and I made Hav very vivid in my own mind, transporting myself there during sleepless nights, drawing pictures of the city during long flights, and finally even writing a book about it. In the way of fiction, though, the place presently developed a disconcerting life of its own, beyond my creation, and my favourite city turned out to have an allegorical side I never planned for it. I never quite discovered what was happening there, beneath the beguiling surface of things, but it seemed that those picturesque ethnic jealousies, which I so enjoyed when I first contrived them, reflected ominous undertones, and were linked with more terrible enmities far away. The city's interesting history, so necessary to my idea of civic completeness, like all interesting histories was not over yet, and when last I inspected the condition of Hav in my mind something very baleful seemed about to happen to the peninsula.

My book created for Hav a modest public around the world. The city has found itself listed in Manguel and Guadalupi's *Dictionary of Imaginary Places* ('a small peninsular city-state in the Near East which boasts many illustrious visitors') and illustrated by diverse artists in magazines and on book jackets. I note though that as often as not *Last Letters from Hav* is stocked on the non-fiction shelves of bookstores, among the travel works, while many of its readers write in true sorrow to ask whose ships they were that I last saw threatening the survival of the City-State. I am unable to answer them, even out of my imagination, and have thus learnt that one cannot heedlessly play about with truth or time. It was no good after all creating a city to my own taste, because art like life has a way of discovering its own endings.

16
Food, Drink and Merriment

I can recall the exact moment, in the Australian summer of 1962, when I became a gastronome. It was a moment less of metamorphosis than of revelation – as though a veil had been lifted from my eyes, a muffle from my tongue, releasing my responses for pleasures I knew not of. I was in my thirties then, and had never taken eating and drinking very seriously. For the most part I simply wanted to get them over with. There may have been something in my family background (we have a Quaker strain to us) which forbade me to enjoy them too much, and anyway I always had more interesting things to do. It had never much worried me when food was bad, and I was never greatly excited when it seemed better than usual.

Everything changed, however, on that Australian summer day. I was being entertained to lunch by an Australian of Hungarian origin, on his garden terrace overlooking Sydney Harbour, looking inland to the bridge. The day was fresh, warm and bright as only an Australian day can be. The harbour glittered. Ships sailed by, the green of the garden was almost unnaturally green and in my memory the flying wings of the Opera House seem to have been soaring with an especially buóyant air of elation.

Into this setting, seductive and half-hallucinatory (for the green was probably no greener than any other, and the Opera House had not been built yet), the Australian brought our lunch. It was nothing elaborate. It was fresh crusty rolls, pâté of some sort, cheese I think, apples and a bottle of local white wine. In substance it was not so different from the family meal I once shared with American evangelists in Afghanistan, which consisted of peanuts and water. Its spirit, though, was not the same. It seemed to me that my friend laid out the plates in the garden purringly, unguently, and when he came to eat the food he did so with a seductive crackling of bread, a voluptuous spreading of pâté, the coolest possible draughting of white wine in the sun. It reminded me of Andrew Marvell:

> What wond'rous life is this I lead!
> Ripe Apples drop about my head!
> The Luscious Clusters of the Vine
> Upon my mouth do crush their Wine . . .

As it happens nobody could be much less pretentious about food and wine than my epicurean host that day, and he would have been astonished to know, as he ate his usual simple lunch before going back to the office, that beside him I was enjoying a moment of new vision; yet so it was, and since then I have approached my victuals with a far less Quakerly dispassion.

The Friends need a Meeting-House to bring out the best in their silence, and for myself I need a restaurant for the full experience of gourmandism. Eating domestically can be fun, can be satisfying, can be technically or artistically excellent, but for me it can never match the rounded ample pleasure of a good meal out. Whether my company has been a lover, a friend, a family party, a group of colleagues or a book – alone or with others, especially since 1962 the stir of the restaurant, the preparatory bustle of the waiters (I am generally the first guest, preferring to go to bed early), the anticipation of the menu and the fulfilment of the dish when the cover is, preferably with a flourish, removed, have all been perennial joys of my life.

I suppose my ideal restaurant is one of the old French bourgeois kind, madame in black bombazine and serious long-aproned garçons pressing on each others' heels out of the kitchen, pursued by herbal fragrances and the clatter of dishes. They are hard to find nowadays, but French restaurants of other categories continue to give me pleasure in the old tradition. My partner and I once spent a week in the French Alps staying in a comfortable family hotel, eating each day gargantuan breakfasts and satisfying suppers, walking the mountains in between. At the end of our stay, driving down to the airport at Geneva, we found ourselves passing Le Père Brise, in those days one of France's supreme restaurants, and scruffy as we were in jeans, boots and anoraks, we decided to stop for lunch.

I shall always remember the welcome they gave us – a table at the lake's edge, a plate of small lake fish with salad, little wild raspberries and a carafe of white wine, served with all possible subtlety of attention. Kindness has always been a speciality of the best French restaurants, and nobody could have been kinder to us than the staff of Le Père Brise (since then alas fallen into harder critical times). We were not in the least affronted, did not in the least regret our little luncheon break, when we found that the cost of it was rather greater than that of our entire week's holiday in the mountains, room, dinners, giant breakfasts and all.

Not kind exactly, but certainly genial is the ambiance of another excruciatingly expensive restaurant I have long been unwisely fond of, the Four Seasons in Manhattan. 'Hey,' cried the busboy to my guest when I took an eminent journalist to lunch there one day, 'hey, great to see ya, you're looking great, how's the game?' – for it turned out, in the American way, that they were members of the same squash club. The Four Seasons occupies one of the very grandest rooms in all New York, in one of the most elegant of all skyscrapers, but it is urbanely relaxed of style. 'Be easy,' Lord Melbourne once told an aspirant politician who sought his advice about tactics, 'I like an easy man.' I agree, and I like an easy restaurant, too.

By now there can be few international celebrities, in any walk of life, who have not had a meal in the Four Seasons' magnificent pool room, so that while unaccustomed guests spend half their time wondering at famous faces, the management oversees its clientele with a worldly lack of excitement, conveying messages here and there, wryly amused by pretension and reasonably tolerant of eccentricity, if sufficiently worldly itself. I was there one day when two amazing women entered with slow purposeful tread, like gangsters in an old movie. They were fiercely made up but dressed all in black, black hats, black dresses, black shoes – stiffened black it seemed to me, as if for some macabre medieval ritual – and heavily, slowly and with a sinister dignity they lowered themselves upon a banquette to survey the room side by side in majesty. The staff observed this stately progress as awestruck as everyone else, but nobody batted an eyelid when an elderly diner at a nearby table, hardly less majestic himself, asked of nobody in particular: '*What d'you suppose they're wearing underneath?*'

Oh, there are many restaurants the very opening of whose doors warm me with the promise of happy hours to come. For forty years and more – yes, since long before my Sydney revelation – I have been catching the experienced eye of the barman at Harry's Bar in Venice, looking up sidelong from opening a bottle or pouring a glass as I push through the famous swing doors. I caught that eye of sophistication somewhat nervously as a young soldier long ago, I caught it all too often when I lived in Venice, I even caught it unawares once when, making a film about the city with a German television crew, I swung into the restaurant preceded by the crouching cameraman, pursued by technicians trailing wires and microphones, and supervised anxiously, as the door closed behind me, by a director in a long black coat with a velvet collar, like Diaghilev. The barman was for once in his life transfixed, the diners stared with scampi on their forks, when we appeared in such wild gallimaufry! In Harry's Bar one night a group of friends and I, being young and heedless, enjoyed our meal so much that we ordered the same thing all over again; twenty years later a woman I met in America said fastidiously that she remembered the occasion well, having watched our performance from the next table.

Of all restaurants I know, the most high-spirited is the Walnut Tree at Llanddewi Skirrid in Wales, a pub in the middle of nowhere whose Italian-Welsh owners have made it famous all over Britain by the excellence and originality of their cuisine. Though hedonists sometimes drive down from London to eat there, it has remained faithful to its tavern origins, and is entirely without sham. This means that its customers, half of them local regulars, treat it as a kind of homely club,. The Welsh waitresses who work there, the young apprentices in the kitchen, old clients eating salmon with rhubarb and casuals who have dropped in for a beer – all are members of the Walnut Tree, and I know of nowhere I would rather go to escape a despondent evening.

Many of the customers come up from Newport, Cardiff and the old coal valleys of South Wales, and they bring with them their own particular dazzle. Often they are rather Italianate of style themselves, a bit showy, loud sometimes, and they are masters and mistresses of pleasure. Eating with true gusto, sharing their laughter among friends and strangers alike, they are like emblematic revellers in an old painting, illustrating nothing disagreeable like Gluttony, but only Conviviality, Hospitality or at worst Self-Indulgence. Often when I am dining there alone these merry people embrace me into their company; and sometimes, the Walnut Tree being what it is, a waitress will make her way over to my table, through the crush and noise of the later evening, to inquire after the children.

Drinking is something else. Drinking for me means only wine, and I did not need my Australian to persuade me of its pleasures. I like to brag that I have drunk a glass of wine every day since the Second World War, and though this is not true in the fact, since I have spent much time in places where there is no wine, it is true in the principle – the chance of war introduced me to wine, and I have never turned away. I believe in wine as I believe in Nature. I cherish its sacramental and legendary meanings, not to mention its power to intoxicate, and just as Nature can be both kind and hostile, so I believe that if bad wine is bad for you, good wine in moderation does nothing but good. If I am ever challenged, I refer people to that seminal work *Wine is the Best Medicine*, in which the great Dr E. A. Maury, pictured on its jacket looking terrifically healthy with a glass of champagne in his hand, prescribes a suitable wine for almost every ailment – Entre-deux-Mers for rickets, young Beaujolais for diarrhoea, two glasses of Sancerre daily to lower the blood pressure . . .

When I was very young I drank, like most of us, with a lack of discrimination and an unvarying enjoyment that I now envy. Thinking of myself then, I am reminded of the great Sherpa mountaineer Tenzing Norkay, whom I witnessed drinking, I rather think, his very first glass of wine of any kind. It was at an official banquet in London. I sat next to the very old-school and gentlemanly functionary who had arranged the occasion, and early in the evening he remarked to me that he hoped I would enjoy the claret, not just the last of its vintage in the official cellars, but perhaps the last in London. I was much impressed, and looked across at Tenzing, who was most certainly enjoying it very much indeed, having as a standard of comparison only the species of alcoholic porridge the

Sherpas call *tsang*. His was a princely figure, and as the lackeys filled and refilled his glass his face shone with pride and pleasure. It was a delight to see him. After a while the old boy on my left turned to me again. 'Oh how good it is to see,' he said with true warmth of approval, 'that Mr Tenzing *knows a decent claret when he has one!*'

My own first wines were all Italian, and nearly all red. The fact that un-Italian wines existed at all was first brought home to me in Port Said, when disembarking from a troopship from Trieste in 1946 I went to a restaurant for dinner with the young commanding officer of my regiment. 'Rhine wine!' exclaimed the colonel in delight – 'after all these years, Rhine wine!' – and though it has since occurred to me that he must have been hardly more than a schoolboy when he had last tasted it, still his savoir-faire made it clear to me that there was more to wine than plonk Chianti.

Since then I have drunk wine of more varieties than my colonel could have conceived. I have drunk Egyptian wines made by Greeks, and Chinese wines made by Frenchmen, and Zimbabwean wines, and Canadian wines, and Peloponnesian draught retsina served in tin bowls, and Scottish wines made from the sap of silver birch trees, and two wines at least that I swear I will never taste again – the Indian-made wine called Colconda and the Kosher Cabernet that is bottled in down-town Manhattan. Believing as I do too in the mythic meaning of wine, its role as a messenger from the *genii locorum*, I have also followed it to some lovely places. In the days when we could still afford to be addicted to the Burgundy called Echézeaux, I once set out to trail the wine from bottle to source, from my wine-rack in Wales to the exact patch of vineyard it came from. I hoped that I would find there some more explicit declaration from the earth-gods – and so I did, for when I drove up the stony track to the half-acre of hill-slope from which every single bottle of Echézeaux has been derived, the solitary French-man working there looked up, saw the Welsh plate on my car and started talking about rugby football.

Wandering the California vineyards led me to the writer M. F. K. Fisher, herself a sort of naiad, whose house stands in the heart of the Napa valley, and whose very presence among her cats, books and cooking implements seemed to me a confirmation of my happiest superstitions. And it was after a generous luncheon in the vineyards of the Cape of Good Hope that I once drove my convertible to the University of Stellenbosch, where I had an appointment to meet the theorists who had given spurious academic respectability to the idea of apartheid. A Cole Porter song called 'True Love' was popular just then, and encouraged by the wine I had drunk, by the beauty of the vineyards, by the grand bowl of the African sky above my head, I was singing this tune at the top of my voice when, skidding to a stop outside the Bureau of Racial Affairs, I found those austere ethnicists awaiting me tight-lipped on the stoep.

But I must admit that the best of all my vinous moments have been with the old Italian red after all. We drank lots of it when we were living in Venice, and sometimes after dinner, if friends were with us, we would take a bottle or two and sail the boat out into the darkness of the lagoon. This was magic. It was not that we were drunk, only that the wine's benevolence had made us better, happier people for the evening, had opened our hearts more receptively to beauty and emotion: so that out there in the purple night, watching the lights of the ships, passing the looming tripods of the sand-bank stakes, and seeing unfolded before us the grand luminosity of Venice itself, its towers and palaces radiant above the viscous water – absorbing all this in wonder and merriment, we really were touched by the gods of the place.

Perhaps they sound gross, these pleasures of food and drink – frequenting extravagant restaurants, eating dinners twice over, singing Cole Porter to monkish racialists, navigating in a semi-inebriated dream among the waters of Venice: but believe me, even as I indulge myself I relish in memory the loaf of crusty bread, the plain plate of pâté, the cheese, the apple and the white wine that changed my life so generously beside the sea in Sydney.

17
Lost Times

Long ago in the village of Llanthony, in the Black Mountains of South Wales, I walked down the road to the telephone box and made one of those calls that so often, in a moment or two of conversation, shapes our destinies. I had just taken my degree at Oxford, and I had been offered two Fleet Street jobs, one rather well paid, the other hardly paid at all. I had already decided which to accept, but even as I walked I allowed myself the chance to change my mind, taking with me the letters from both newspapers in case of divine revelations on the way. Nothing happened, though; I reached the red call-box (Button A to be pressed when you got through to your destination, Button B to get your money back if you failed), asked the operator for a Trunk Call to Central 2000, and committed myself to a career with *The Times*, London's oldest, most famous and worst-paying newspaper.

In the event the career was short, five years only, but it was wonderfully entertaining. It sent me to America for a year, to Egypt for a couple more, to India and all over the Arab world. It afforded me, at one time or another, a riverside flat in Hammersmith, a houseboat on the Nile, part of an ante-bellum mansion in Vicksburg, a green Chevrolet, an MG and a pretty white Rover. It affected my attitudes for ever. Start to finish, trainee sub-editor to Middle East Correspondent, *The Times* never paid me more than £1,200 a year, but I prize my association with this most fascinating of all newspapers more than millions.

When I joined it *The Times* was half-marooned by history. Though it had begun its career, in the 1780s, as a knockabout London broadsheet in competition with many others, during the nineteenth-century it had become a unique national institution, almost an organ of State, the mouthpiece of an English ruling class which was still all-confident and cohesive. Foreigners often assumed it to be an instrument of Government, interpreting its editorials as official leaks and suspecting its foreign correspondents as intelligence agents. Its in-house jokes and postures were framed to emphasize its uniqueness, and the very look of the paper, with nothing but small advertisements on its front page and a stately royal crest at its masthead, seemed to imply that it was nothing to do with Fleet Street at all.

By 1951 all this was fast being overtaken. The Second World War had shaken many of the paper's assumptions. Socialist government had threatened many more. A discredited record on Munich had weakened old claims to omniscience. The English ruling class was disintegrating, and the ideal of an exclusive, highly civilized elite was no longer respectable. The paper I joined accordingly had to it a slight air of pastiche, as it groped its way towards a more contemporary identity; I was only just in time to know it when its personality was still *sui generis*, before it rejoined the ranks of the everyday Press.

The Times then occupied the same site, Printing House Square near Blackfriars Bridge, upon which it had started life. During my first weeks with the paper I worked in the sub-editors' room, overlooking Queen Victoria Street, and promptly at the same time each evening I would hear the tramp of marching feet outside our window. It was a picket of the Brigade of Guards marching up to the Bank of England to mount guard on the national treasure, followed all the way by a slow-revving fifteen-cwt truck carrying, I assume, the rations and the ammunition. New as I was to London life, this nightly passage made me feel almost arcanely close to the sources of tradition, and when I came away from the window and looked around me at my workplace, the illusion was only heightened, for Printing House Square seemed to me then a very ark of Englishness.

The building itself was a beguiling warren of bits and pieces, mostly Victorian or older, stuck together with bridges, corridors, alleyways and ancient elevators, and grouped asymmetrically around the Square itself, which had a single tree in it, a small patch of grass behind a railing, and a pub called the Lamb and

Lark. *The Times* produced an exquisite cloth-bound monograph about Printing House Square, 140 pages long, printed *in situ* on hand-made paper, illustrated with maps, inserted prints, engravings and facsimile documents, and limited to 100 copies for private circulation (mine is number nineteen).

Except for the printing machines, which were very modern, almost nothing in this establishment was up-to-date. From the editor's elderly Rolls-Royce to the filing systems of the Intelligence Department, all seemed to be of yesteryear. The ramrod commissioner who stood guard in the front hall wore the medal ribbons of the First World War. Coal fires burned in the rooms of the leader-writers. Scholarly specialists stalked the corridors, an eminent authority on early English water-colours, the former Prime Minister of an Indian State, a constitutional expert who, since he happened also to be Arundel Herald Extraordinary, was to be seen on days of State ceremony dressed up like a playing-card. Peter Fleming the celebrated explorer often wrote his humorous editorials in the library, and littérateurs of many kinds earned a useful living among the sub-editors. I myself had been recruited by Stanley Morison, the shadowy typographer, historian and grey eminence of the paper.

To this unusual ambience I most happily adapted. The whole institution seemed to me a kind of historical dream. I bought myself (staff rate) the first two volumes of Morison's gigantic unfinished history, and found them peopled with eccentrics, grandees, adventurers and intellectuals of astonishing variety. What a paper, I thought – the people who wrote it were at least as interesting as the people they wrote about, and the Brigade of Guards itself marched by its door each evening!

Forty years later my months at Printing House Square seem almost mythical. Could it really be true that I dined each evening in an eighteenth-century office dining-room, served by a butler and offered snuff from an enamelled box with a picture of St Petersburg on it? Did the foreign news editor really assure me that, if I were ever to be killed in the service of the paper, I could be certain of a decent obituary? Am I romancing, or did I truly hear Eric Shipton the mountaineer, discussing the prospects of representing *The*

Times in Latin America, say in all seriousness that he could not of course live in a city, but would have to be based in the Andes somewhere?

Certainly the exclusive items of news that came into my hands, during my time as assistant to the foreign news editor, were sometimes gloriously in character. For instance I was the first to hear, in a cable from South Africa, that the coelecanth had been rediscovered in the ocean depths – I had to go to Iolo Williams, the water-colour expert, to find out what a coelecanth was – and I was the first to learn, from a telephone call, that the Cretan script called Linear B had been deciphered. Sometimes people of great dignity but less importance, retired ambassadors, exiled politicians, distinguished but unheard-of academics, would arrive at the front office demanding to see the Foreign Editor; often enough they were palmed off with me, twenty-five years old, and it was I who became privy to their esoteric political gossip or theories of economic stagnation.

Here are two of my favourite stories about Printing House Square. They may not be very funny in themselves, but their tone and temper evokes in me the fustian magic of my time in that place. In the first the paper's dramatic critic, finding himself in a theatre that is burnt down in the course of a play's first night, turns in a perfectly straightforward critique of the performance, remarking only that he cannot comment upon the ending, because the theatre burnt down during Act 3. The editor sends him a gentle note next day, suggesting that if such a thing happens another time, he might contribute a brief report on the calamity to the news pages. 'My dear editor,' the critic replies, 'you seem to be under a misapprehension as to the nature of my employment with *The Times*. I am your Dramatic Critic, not your *news-hound*.'

In the second story an editorial writer is asked to prepare a leader about educational reforms in Bosnia. According to his custom he has the fire in his room well-stacked, and a bottle of port sent up to ease the task. However not having made a particular study of the Bosnian school curricula, he finds it hard to get started, and presently sends for another bottle. The hours pass. The life of the paper proceeds inexorably towards press time. A messenger is sent to ask how the leader is coming along, and opening the door of the writer's well-warmed room, discovers the following scene. Both bottles of port are empty. The leader-writer is fast asleep in his chair. And in his exquisite handwriting on the sheet of paper in front of him – as far as he has got in expressing *The Times*'s view on educational progress in Sarajevo, is a single well-considered word:

'Nevertheless'.

Presently they sent me away to be a foreign correspondent, and at a distance from Printing House Square working for *The Times* became a proper contemporary occupation. Presently, too, *The Times* itself uncertainly escaped from its own spell. News appeared on the front page, that glorious old office was demolished, all the new technologies were adopted and as the years passed the newspaper became more or less like all others. It was inevitable, and probably high time too.

I love the old style, though. I cherish its absurdities still, and admire the humour which ran through even the most pompous of the paper's attitudes. When I was representing *The Times* abroad I was once invited by an advertising agency to take part in a publicity campaign, promoting a Swiss-made typewriter. *Times* correspondents were strictly anonymous in those days, so I sent a cable to Printing House Square asking if acceptance of the offer would be disastrous to my future with the paper. Back came a reply instantly, square and simple: YES STOP DISASTROUS STOP TIMES.

I filed it for ever affectionately in my memory, along with the coelecanth, the snuff-box and Nevertheless.

18
French Dreams

France has been a consolation of my life, and one reason is a strange sensation of clarity that affects me there. It is a selective clarity. I constantly confuse French towns and cities, I forget from one year to the next in which department I have been, and at least one French river of my mind is not in France at all. Although I go there nearly every year, sometimes two or three times, my feelings about the country are less choate than they are about other places, and harder to pin down. In matters of petty detail, however, in everyday episodes and the observation of passing scenes, somehow in France I seem to see things at once more clearly and more puzzlingly – as in one of those dreams whose meanings are enigmatic, but whose events and characters are preternaturally precise. Here are a few examples, recalled from four very different parts of the country – I forget exactly where.

Somewhere from the warm south first. I stayed once at a hotel on a slope of the aromatic hills east of the Rhône, and my cameo concerns an Algerian who was employed there as gardener and handyman, cleaning the swimming-pool in the mornings, rearranging the chaises longues on the terrace, cutting the grass on the lawn which was not really a lawn at all, but just a patch of the rough grassland all around.

It was not a grand hotel: a middle rank hotel, *très confortable* in the Michelin guide, with a red rocking-chair for peace and quiet. Its owner, however, was extremely elegant. He wore a boutonnière every day of the year, he seemed to know all there was to know abut the newer cuisines, being his own chef, and he encouraged local artists, if sufficiently modernist (none of your tourist trash) to exhibit their works in his corridors. He had a wife, I was led to believe, but she did not show: only this urbane host, supported by sundry girls and two young waiters who, arriving early in the morning to serve breakfast, awoke us all with the roar of their motor-bikes up the winding road from the village.

My fellow guests were not especially grand either. A few foreigners had been brought there, like me, by the Michelin entry, but most of the clients were local lawyers, doctors and their wives, or business people of the more fastidious kind. Some were restauranteurs on their evening off, and these were welcomed with particular charm by the proprietor, not I suspect because they were colleagues, but because they made him feel superior. On summer afternoons there were usually two or three families splashing about in the pool, and sometimes one heard the plonk of tennis-balls from the unkempt asphalt court beyond the trees.

Such was the hotel, and through it night and day moved the Algerian. He was an extremely tall man – he towered above the hotelier – but cadaverous. His cheeks were sunken wolfishly, and since he was always unshaven, without being actually bearded, and his eyes blazed in their deep sockets, he looked at first sight rather sinister. He loped wolfishly, too, but very slowly, stalking here and there, pushing wheelbarrows or carrying garden tools, silently appearing in the corners of one's eye when one least expected him. Sometimes he simply stood at the end of the terrace beyond the dining-room, staring at us all from a distance, and he looked then like a resentful slave.

Perhaps he sounds disturbing, but actually his most striking characteristic was his fine balding forehead. His hair had receded only in the middle, leaving him almost luxuriant sideburns, and this gave him a noble scholarly aspect. He was like a professor in some medieval academy of Islam. If from a distance he suggested a morosely brooding captive, at close quarters I used to imagine towering preoccupations of art or principle to be engaging his mind. As he trundled his barrow about, surely he was debating within himself subtle mathematical formulae, or composing Sufi couplets? *Lost is the Dewdrop with the morning sun* (I fancied him thinking) *Save only within the Petals of the Rose*!

Every morning at breakfast-time, when the first guests came down to the terrace, the Algerian was to be seen cleaning the pool below. But he had been up for hours by then. Once after a disturbed night I got up myself at the very break of day, long before the waiters arrived, and walking up the hill behind the hotel I came across him among the outbuildings at the edge of the property, where it petered away into wilderness. He was feeding a black and white cat. He stood very erect above the animal, having placed a tin dish of offal before it, and I heard him murmuring endearments to the creature. They sounded stately endearments, like Koranic blessings, and he stood there gauntly, as the sun rose behind him, looking down at the cat and murmuring.

Clearly the cat hardly liked to begin eating, in these circumstances. It kept circling around the Algerian's feet, casting glances at the food, rubbing its head against the man's ankles, until it felt it had paid its proper respects; only then did it fall, with snarls and rendings through its purrs, upon the unlovely victuals.

Next I remember a moment in one of those middle-sized provincial towns, almost anywhere in the French interior, which still have a military flavour, with a barracks on the outskirts and bars where soldiers hang out. In a square not quite in the middle of this particular example – not the chief square with the town hall and the car parks, but a lesser one around the corner, with two cafés in it, and lime trees stooped over a news kiosk, where only an occasional car, olive-green army truck or motor-bike went by, rather too fast – at a table outside one of those cafés three girls sat over Coca-Colas in the early evening. I can see them now, vivid against the torpid activity of the café behind, which consisted of a couple of men reading newspapers separately in the late sunshine, bending intently over their papers like jewellers over trays, and an unhealthy-looking woman in green, balding at the back of her head, confiding something in low tones to the owner at the bar.

The girls were drably dressed, in T-shirts and jeans, but heavily made up. Their lips were full and crimson, and there were applications of pink, purple and even orange around their eyes. I imagine they would like to have been punks, if they could have got away with it in such a town. They talked and laughed loudly, breaking off to take long pulls through their straws, but I could tell that they were bored. They laughed by rote, by custom. Their eyes strayed.

One of them complained that her right ear, lately pierced, was hurting her, but the other sympathized only in a stylized way. Their sandals hung loosely from their feet, which they sometimes jiggled suddenly up and down beneath the table, as though in time to an inaudible and sporadic pulse.

Around the corner came four young soldiers. They were in civilian clothes, more or less what the girls were wearing, but they were unmistakably soldiers all the same. They had come off duty an hour or two before, I guessed, and had slicked themselves up for the evening. How pale they looked! Their hair was cropped cruelly short, and they had a scrubbed, boiled and blistered appearance. They must have been very recent conscripts, enduring their first few awful weeks upon the parade ground. Their faces were drawn, as though from fear of sergeant-majors, and I thought how their poor mothers would fret, if they could see their children then.

The recruits swung noisily into the café yard, smoking cigarettes, and took chairs at the next table to the girls. They were extremely self-conscious, and full of bravado. One of them leant across and pretended to flick his cigarette ash into a girl's Coke. The others, jostling as it were for place, laughed raucously, scraping the chairs about, and made as if to join the girls, leaning back in their seats and offering salacious comments – they talked throatily, very fast and almost unintelligibly, as if coming from unknown provinces.

But as if to a signal, without a word, the girls rose from their places and walked in line abreast from the café. They swung their bodies provocatively as they disappeared across the square, and bending their heads to each other, exchanged remarks which we all knew to be derisory. They did not giggle. They merely walked away. The soldiers, left to themselves, lapsed into silence, and sprawled around their table in a newly relaxed way. Suddenly they seemed very tired. With a burbling crackle a moped entered the square, ridden by a young woman in a crash helmet. The heads of the recruits turned in parallel to watch her pass, but without much interest.

To the Biscay coast now. One day I sat on a promenade there, preparing a picnic for myself and looking at the view, which was, without being particularly beautiful, bright and invigorating. Yachts sailed about, flying gay pennants. In the bay eight or nine dinghies were being marshalled by a sailing instructor, and his voice reached me muffled and distorted through his megaphone. In silhouette out at sea there stood some sort of oil rig or floating dock, something not quite a ship, spiked and bulky on the horizon. I could hear children laughing somewhere out of sight.

To my right a jetty protruded into the sea, and around it there presently came into my field of view a swimming man. Festive though the scene in general was, there was nothing celebratory about him. He was in his fifties, I would guess, stout but muscular. He wore a rubber cap on his head, and he was swimming, with an absolute rhythmic exactitude, a slow and powerful crawl. One, two, one, two, deep-wallowing in the water went his head, up came his podgy arm, out emerged his face for breath, running with salt-water – a slight pause at the top of his stroke, and he was down again half-submerged, the sea rising and falling about him, reminding me of sailing-ships in old pictures deep in the troughs of oceans.

His movements were utterly disciplined. He never wavered. The pace of his stroke was metronomic, and suddenly it occurred to me that he was on a *voyage*. He was a swimmer on his way somewhere, as one might walk to work, or take a bus. He was the first swimmer I ever saw who was using his crawl as a means of transport. I watched him intently while I munched my food, and once I thought I caught his eye, as he rolled around for breath out there; but if I did, it was an entirely dispassionate eye, like the lense of a submarine's periscope.

It took him some time to pass me, until eventually he disappeared around the headland to my left; and for some time afterwards I fancied I could hear the regular flop and splashing of his stroke, as one sometimes hears the tread of a ship's engines when it has long sailed out of vision. Since then, whenever I hear such a beat of engines in the night, I think, there goes the French swimmer, on his way.

Finally I record an episode in a small market town in the very centre of France, where I stopped one morning to buy myself some toothpaste. Because it was market day, I had to join a queue of people waiting for prescriptions to be filled at the pharmacist's. Through the shop's tinted window the bustle of the market showed, the movement of ungainly rib-sided vans, the unrolling of awnings, clothes hanging from racks, heads passing this way and that, and I could hear shouting sometimes, and the revving of engines.

Inside everything was different. Like all French pharmacists, the shop was austerely up-to-date. There were electronic devices of several kinds behind the counter, all grey and white, with paper scrolling out of printers, and a computer screen greenish in a corner. The filing system was of grey steel, its drawers moving on almost silent rollers. Not a bottle could be seen. On the counter there were only one or two displays of shampoos and medicinal soaps, dummies I suspect. The atmosphere was hushed, and the line of customers, mostly elderly and well wrapped up, waited in silence as though to show respect for all this technique.

Behind the counter the young pharmacist and his wife, both in white coats, were quietly preparing medicines, summoning data from disks, checking the computer screen, rolling those soundless drawers. It seemed almost a betrayal of the times, when they had to wrap a box of pills in perfectly ordinary paper, even though they did seal it with deft manipulations of Scotch tape from a dispenser. They talked to their customers in undertones, and the clients in turn accepted their medicines with murmured thanks and walked quietly away, sometimes nodding a greeting, no more, to acquaintances in the queue. Whenever the shop door was opened it allowed inside, for a moment or two, a sudden clash of noises, smells and colours from the market.

Well after 9.30 the pharmacist's assistant arrived, flustered because she was late. The queue eyed her as she hurried by. She took off her raincoat, hanging it in a cupboard, put on a white overall, tidied her hair hastily in a mirror, and joined her employers at the prescription counter. As she did so the pharmacist, moving to the other end of the counter, quite deliberately bumped her with his elbow. Everybody saw it. All the women in the queue took note of it. The pharmacist's wife saw it. There was nothing furtive about it. It was an open, calculated bump. It seemed to me like a message, to which everyone but me was a privy. The assistant, I noticed, looked rather surly as she took the impact. The pharmacist's wife stared stony-faced, first at her husband, then at the girl.

The silence of the customers became a watchful, waiting silence, but nothing more happened, and soon the assistant too was busily checking, calculating and expertly detaching strips of adhesive tape.

What could it mean? Were the pharmacist and his assistant having an affair? Was his passion of the night before the cause of her lateness in the morning? The bump might have been a nudge, an acknowledgement of past delights, a hint of lusts to come. If so, then the wife must surely be complicit to the liaison, and so also must be many of the customers – who must have known, I felt sure, not only the assistant, but the boss himself, and his cool, contemporary, self-controlled, probably Paris-educated wife since they were children. Ah, I thought to myself, the flying of time, the old stories!

But on the other hand perhaps they particularly disliked each other, the chemist and his assistant? The bump might just as easily have been a vicious little blow, intended to hurt. The wife's glance might have been saying yes, quite right, the idle little bitch, you show her! When my turn came to reach the counter it was the assistant who chanced to serve me, but her eyes told me nothing as she handed me my toothpaste, and behind her employers had their heads together over a print-out.

An old fellow in a quilted fur-collared jacket left the shop just before me, and feeling by now in a busy-body mood, I followed him down the market street. I thought he might afford some clues about the incident within – I might find him laughing disagreeably about it with a friend, or alternatively shaking his head in regret. But instead he did something almost stagily French. He walked around the corner at the end of the street, where two open-air pissoirs were fixed to the walls, and relieved himself in silence. I returned to the car and drove on.

I realize, of course, that one can see such things anywhere, soldiers and swimmers, love or spitefulness, a man feeding a cat as the sun comes up; but in the light of France, somehow or other, they reveal themselves differently to me – as I say, like one of those dreams.

102

19
Fisher's Face

When people ask me why there is a portrait on my wall of the late Admiral Lord Fisher of Kilverstone, with his signature cut from a letter and stuck below, together with a piece of wood alleged to be from the quarterdeck of Nelson's *Victory*, I tell them it is because in the next life he and I are going to have an affair. The picture is a *Spy* cartoon, circa 1910, and whenever I make this preposterous and perhaps blasphemous claim I look up to see how the admiral is taking it. Slyly, a little sourly, amused and knowing he looks back at me, his mouth turned down at the corners in a curdled smile, and I know that he does not mind. 'Think in oceans, sink at sight,' he liked to say, and he is sure to approve of such an unblushing, straight-from-the-shoulder claim upon posterity.

I have been in love with him for nearly forty years. That he died six years before I was born, that he was in many ways an appalling person and in other ways a fool, does not in the least moderate my passion. When Fisher was Commander-in-Chief of the Royal Navy's Mediterranean Fleet, in 1901, the Sultan of Morocco was invited to visit him upon his flagship *Renown*, and was given a tour of the vessel. What, he was asked afterwards, had most impressed him about the visit – the great 10-inch guns in their barbettes, the mighty 12,000-horsepower engines, the armoured conning-tower, the torpedo tubes? The Sultan did not hesitate for a moment. 'The Admiral's face,' he said.

So it was with me. The moment I first saw 'Jacky' Fisher's face, photographed in a book of naval history, I knew he was my man. Because one half of me would like to be him, and the other half would like to be loved by him, he had come over the years to assume an allegorical part in my consciousness; and so I place him now affectionately in the centre of this book, whose every page expresses, if only between the lines, much the same ambivalence.

The face did not radically change through all the years of the Admiral's career, midshipman on the China Station in the last of the opium wars to First Sea Lord at Whitehall in the Great War of 1914–18. Its outlines always looked much the same. It was a round face, slightly oriental of cast – fanciful legend claimed that, Fisher being the son of a tea planter in Ceylon, his mother was a Congalese princess. While its eyes were frank, boyish and often slightly surprised, its mouth was eminently sardonic. It was a mouth made for sceptical amusement, and as the years passed it developed only in intensity; the mischievous twist of boyhood became the arrogant half-sneer of the post-captain, and finally the megalomaniac leer, frozen in theatrical disdain, of the superannuated Admiral of the Fleet. He was always vastly entertained by life – he loved merriment, youth, display, Edward VII, sermons and dancing, if necessary humming his own waltz music; but when he grew old fame, power and disappointment soured the enjoyment, and made a mask of those magnificent features.

My picture on the stairs, though euphemized rather, shows Fisher more or less as the Sultan saw him, at the happy and all-confident summit of his powers. I dare say there has never been a young admiral of the Royal Navy so exuberantly sure of himself, or more romantically intoxicated by his profession. In an age of convention, in a traditional service, Fisher was one of a kind. Some thought him crazy, and I suspect he really did believe himself to be a reincarnation of Nelson. He was nominated for the navy, he loved to say, by the last of Nelson's captains; his first ship was *Victory*, in which he later flew his admiral's flag; he became First Sea Lord on one Trafalgar Day, he published his memoirs on another; and it was perhaps no coincidence that he spent his last days in the bosom of Nina, Duchess of Hamilton.

He believed in favouritism – the notorious Fishpond was his equivalent of Nelson's Band of Brothers – and perhaps in the end it was this proclivity, together with a daring taste for innovation, that permanently embittered that mouth. If Fisher was the cleverest officer in the navy of his day, he was also certainly the most resented. His nepotism antagonized those left outside the circle, his bold new ideas upset officers of the old school, his free-and-easy social views distressed those who thought of the navy's officer caste as a club for like-minded gentlemen. He was a shameless wire-puller, assiduous in making useful contacts in industry, aristocracy and the Press. He was terrifically indiscreet. He was at once exhibitionist and sycophantic in his friendship with Edward VII, and all too freely dropped anecdotes about Queen Victoria's dinner-parties ('What were you saying to your neighbours, Captain Fisher, that amused them so much?' 'I was just telling them, ma'am, that I had enough flannel wound around my tummy to go around the walls of this room.')

He could also be faithless, malicious, childish and egotistical. And yet I have his picture on my wall! Well, but he made up for his weaknesses by his overwhelming charm, intelligence and style, and by his devotion to the institution that was his passion and his pride. His own sailors adored him. Years ago I proposed to write his biography, and wrote letters to several newspapers soliciting personal memories. The aged seamen who responded, and the widows of men who had been in Fisher's crews, wrote one and all with a touching affection for his memory. Sometimes they sent me letters the Admiral himself had written, to stokers or able seamen, of a truer sincerity than the flamboyant opportunistic scrawls he loved to send to statesmen, industrialists or influential journalists. He was usually very kind to his juniors, and his zest for life infected all ranks – shipboard dancing was compulsory on his vessels, quarterdecks being especially adapted as dance floors. Those who admired him learnt to accept his streak of cruelty, and there were many officers of character who knew how to deal with him. For instance his second-in-command in the Mediterranean, receiving an insolent summons from his Commander-in-Chief, replied grimly: 'I am on my way, *and wearing my frock-coat and sword*' – the kind of talk Fisher appreciated.

Fisher loved and respected women, and they adored him. They did not have to suffer the barbs of his rivalry, and from boyhood he was a post-master at pleasing them. To his plump and homely wife ('Darling Heart') he was more or less loyal to the end, and we see her once entertaining guests in his admiral's cabin on *Renown* looking for all the world as though she is having the archdeacon's wife to tea. To other women he was irresistibly attentive: to the otherwise forgotten Mrs Edmund Warden ('Dearest Mams') who befriended him as a midshipman in Shanghai, to Queen Victoria, who frequently invited him down to Osborne, to Queen Alexandra ('Your Sweet Majesty'), to the Duchess of Hamilton, his eponymous substitute for Nelson's Emma, who sat at his bedside when he died, and thought he had inherited 'the mantle of Nelson but his spirit increased ten-fold'. It was partly his self-satisfaction, I do not doubt, that beguiled them as it beguiles me. He was so wonderfully full of himself. We see him as a young captain, legs crossed in a posed portrait, looking as though he would happily have taken on an enemy fleet single-handed; we see him as commander of Portsmouth dockyard, feet apart, stick in hand, cap tilted back, looking as jovial and swaggering as a publican; we see him in Jacob Epstein's portrait head, done in the Admiral's extreme old age, looking like an oriental despot, bedizened with orders and maniacally haughty. His shipboard entertainments were lavish, and his ship was always the smartest, the slickest and preferably the most powerful on the station. To those who had only his own word for his accomplishments he must have seemed, as he evidently seemed to the Sultan of Morocco, the very embodiment of British naval confidence.

But panache and rodomontade apart, Fisher really was an innovator of genius, one of the great organizing admirals of naval history. He saw very little action in his life – none at all after the bombardment of Alexandria in 1882 – but in effect he created, as First Sea Lord, the navy which saw Great Britain safely through the First World War. By his example, by his ideas and by his often ruthless practice he had changed it from an imperial exhibition to a modern fighting force. He raised the status of its engineer officers, hitherto scarcely seen as true officers at all. He transformed its standards of gunnery. He introduced the water-tube boiler, 'the fire where the water used to be and the water where the fire used to be'. He instituted the fateful change from coal to oil, and engineered the acquisition of Persian oil fields to supply it. He was the father of the turbine-powered *Dreadnought*, the first all-big-gun battleship, which in 1911 made all other capital ships obsolete, and gave its name to an entire class of fighting ships all over the world. Not perhaps until Admiral Hyman Rickover, USN, presided over the birth of the nuclear submarine, had such fateful advances in naval architecture been achieved by one man's vision. When Fisher, aged seventy-three, was recalled from retirement in 1914 to be First Sea Lord to Churchill's First Lord of the Admiralty, the whole nation was cheered by the news; and Fisher himself must have felt that his life was about to be fulfilled with a truly Nelsonian majesty.

It was not to be – his life ended in tragic bathos; but then it is not in his moments of triumph that I myself most love Jack Fisher, but in his moments of poignant failure. In the early years of the Great War he hoped to be the organizing genius behind another and still grander Trafalgar, an annihilating victory which would utterly eliminate Britain's enemies from the sea. He believed in the most aggressive strategies. He thought the Royal Navy ought to land an army on the Baltic coast of Germany, to make straight as a bullet for Berlin, and actually started work on a fleet of fast warships of low draft to take it there. When three British cruisers were lost off the Chilean coast in 1915, in a stroke of genuinely Nelsonian decision he sent two brand-new battlecruisers, so fresh from the yards that some of the workmen were still on board, instantly to the Falkland Islands to destroy the German squadron in revenge. He was all for speed, range, surprise, thinking in oceans and sinking at sight.

It was hardly surprising then that at first he enthusiastically supported the notion of a purely naval attack upon the Dardanelles, to get at Germany through its Turkish flank. He even seemed prepared to abandon his Baltic project in its favour. However by the end of March, 1915, the Royal Navy had failed in its attempt to force the Narrows and overwhelm the Turks by sheer superbia. Armies were landed instead, but they too failed to breach the Turkish defences, and found themselves helplessly bogged down on the coast of Gallipoli. Six British battleships were sunk or crippled, ever more naval reinforcements were demanded, and suddenly, in an old man's way, Fisher lost heart. He refused to commit more forces to the Dardenalles, and was ready to sacrifice his office and his reputation rather than more of his ships and men – '*I really don't think I can stand it.*'

On a Saturday morning he sent in his resignation, and without waiting for its acceptance or rejection, disappeared, leaving nobody in his place. Couriers scoured London, bearing messages ordering him in the King's name to remain at his post, but for several crucial hours, while the entire conduct of the war hung in the balance, he was nowhere to be found. When they tracked him down at last, to a room at the Charing Cross Hotel, he laid down six preposterous conditions upon which he would stay in office, including the sacking of the entire Board of Admiralty and his own appointment to 'absolutely untrammelled sole command of all sea forces whatsoever'. He was perhaps suffering a nervous breakdown. At this very moment there came intelligence that the German High Seas fleet was about to sail from its bases, and that the ultimate sea-battle was perhaps about to be fought. Still Fisher (who believed the Germans were simply exercising) refused to return to his responsibilities. Asquith the Prime Minister thought he ought to be shot. The King thought he should be hanged at the yard-arm. Queen Alexandra wrote: '*Stick* to your *Post* like *Nelson!*' But he never went back to the Admiralty, instead taking the train to Scotland to fall for ever into his Duchess's arms.

This miserable conclusion to a grand career has always haunted me, and in particular the missing hours on the fateful Saturday of his resignation. Nobody knows for sure where he went, but the chances are that he spent the morning in Westminster Abbey, a favourite refuge of his (he was a deeply religious man – 'I thought it would be a good thing to be a missionary, but I thought it would be better to be First Sea Lord.') There in the half-darkness I fancy I can see him, hunched in his pew, hair white by now, face already fixed and jowly, muttering to himself I dare say as he rehearsed his half-deranged claims and grievances, and seeing through the tears of his mind's eye the sunken ships and drowned people of the Dardanelles. I wish I had been there to comfort him.

For it is the pathos of Fisher that most attracts me to him. Although as it happened he was right about the Dardanelles – right too in believing that the High Seas Fleet was *not* out to battle that day –

the nation never did, as he continued to hope, call him back to its service. He never achieved his Trafalgar, his protégés in command of the Royal Navy's Grand Fleet failing to win the supreme victory he had planned. His dream-ships, the lightly-armoured, powerfully gunned, immensely fast battle-cruisers, proved less than invincible after all ('there's something wrong with my bloody battle-cruisers,' said Beatty of them at Jutland), and reached a tragic dénouement twenty years after Fisher's death with the destruction of HMS *Hood*, the most magnificent of them all, by a single German shell in the next war.

But then Fisher was, I suspect, always more vulnerable than he allowed. There was something wrong with him, too. His younger brother Frederick, who was known variously as 'Uncle Bill' and 'Jacky Fisher's hot-water bottle', also became an admiral, but being less possessed by ambition and less gifted with genius, seems to have been a much happier man. Fisher himself was always playing a part. His marvellous handwriting, tremendously bold and enriched with numberless exclamation marks, underlinings and capital letters, was surely too spontaneous to be true. His aphorisms and quotations, writ so large and so frequently repeated, were more like mantras than *bons mots* – 'Yours till hell freezes', 'The essence of war is immoderation', 'Rashness in war is prudence', 'Reiteration is the secret of conviction', 'Time and the Ocean and some Guiding Star/In High Cabal have made us what we are'. The older he got, the more egotistical were his views, and the more outlandish his style became. In his last years he took to writing endless letters to *The Times*, scrawled eccentrically this way and that, in many variations of his by then almost illegible calligraphy. Wickham Steed, the editor, responded to them kindly enough, but rather patronizingly, as it might be to an aged invalid, for by then Fisher had become one of those deluded patriots who believe that single-handed they can save the nation, if only the nation will see it. His prophetic vision remained astonishing – he accurately foresaw the development of air power, and of submarine warfare – but so absurdly conceited had he grown, so embarrassing to his former colleagues, that when in 1918 the German High Seas Fleet surrendered to the Royal Navy he had created, Fisher was not invited to the ceremony.

I never did write that biography, but in nearly all my books I have made mention of Jack Fisher, as my personal small tribute to his memory. His letters have often made me laugh with delight, his bold schemes and unquenchable flow of ideas enthrall me. Even his ill-will at least makes excellent reading. But above all it is still the look of him that brings his shade so close to me. Long ago I was at Marianske Lazne, in Czechoslovakia, a spa which as Marienbad in the old Austria-Hungary had been one of Fisher's favourite watering-places (besides being agreeably soigné its waters were good for his rheumatism). When I was there Czechoslovakia was in the gloomiest depths of Stalinism, and the town was run by Party thugs, but I asked nevertheless if there was likely to be anyone around who would remember English visitors from before the First World War. It was possible, said the louts. The woman who worked as cleaner at the civic museum, whose villa it had once been and who now lived in its basement, might be sufficiently old and capitalist. They rudely summoned her from below, and she came wiping her hands on her apron, dressed almost in rags and moving rather stiffly, as though she had suffered a stroke. 'Here she is,' they said, 'ask her what you want.' I was embarrassed and angry, and wished I had never brought the old lady into this brutal limelight, but I inquired nevertheless if she had by any chance come across, in former times, Admiral Sir John Fisher of the Royal Navy?

Her answer was immediate, short and convincing. 'Jacky Fisher!' she said. 'What a face that man had.'

20
On Astringency

Let us consider the astringent pleasures. To astringe, I see from the dictionary, means to bind together, and for myself I do often prefer the tightening, clenching pleasures to the let-it-all-out kind – kirsch with my strawberries, Georgian before baroque, north on the whole rather than south, cats not dogs, goats before sheep, tea more than coffee, plain chocolate rather than milk. I like the insinuating numbers – the threes, the fives, the sevens, the nines – more than the robust sixes and eights that the Chinese think lucky. I thought it was very good for me when, having delivered at a public reading in Los Angeles one of the very purplest of my purple passages, all about the golden glimmer and incense of the Basilica at Venice, a young American in the front row popped up the moment I finished with a distinctly deflationary question: "'Scuse me, d'ya have to pay to get into that church?'

W. H. Auden used to quote an unnamed Oxford don as saying that he was 'not quite happy about pleasure', and I suppose he meant that it generally lacked *gravitas*. Perhaps, like so many people, he found satisfaction chiefly in conflict, if only dialectical. I hate quarrelling, which clearly gives delight to some, and despise grumbling, which is almost a hobby for many more, but I certainly get a quivering satisfaction out of danger. Zoos are among the things that most easily move me to fury, and when I was invited once to contribute to an anthology of Hate, with immense pleasure I offered the following malediction:

I cast a curse upon zoos.
I curse their smug hypocritical directors, spouting

111

conservationist cant among their dungeons.
I curse their mindless keepers, throwing quips to the
children as they bar the gates of perpetual confinement.
I curse their veterinary surgeons, sterilizing the instruments
of mercy in the house of unending cruelty.
I curse their technicians, peering through
electronic eyes at the intimacies of their prisoners.
I curse their collectors, who are the children of the slave
traders.
I curse their geneticists, who are the brood of Auschwitz.
I curse their Friends and Life Members, whose
subscriptions are the wages of evil.
I call down the hate of heaven and hell upon them all: may the
anathema of the ages fall upon their heads to consume them,
and may the divine lightning, even as it strikes the locks
from their foul pits and cages, shrivel them in shame and
ignominy.

Of course it is only self-righteous anger that can give one true pleasure. I expect many a dedicated Fellow of the Royal Zoological Society, reading this cant, will get a certain frisson out of execrating me.

When the Caliph Omar accepted the surrender of Jerusalem from the Patriarch Sophronius, he rode into the fallen city on a snow-white camel, but was dressed all in rags to emphasize the Prophet's creed of poverty. I have always admired Islam for the continuing simplicity and egalitarianism of its style, honouring Mohammed's values far more faithfully than Christians honour those of Jesus, and in a figurative way I often feel better myself for an hour or two of extreme asceticism. This I most easily achieve by getting myself drenched to the skin on a mountain. It is a poor substitute for a life of epic abstinence, like Omar's, but it is something. Nowhere can be much wetter than a wet Welsh mountain, and when I am really soaked through up there I feel that I have been utterly absorbed into the geological, climactical, historical, psycho-logical and spiritual damp of the place. The rain seems to drop from the clouds directly down my neck beneath my several layers of clothing to the small of my back. The wet wind embraces every part of me like an anti-insulation. Tears from the sky, tears from my eyes, tears of history stream conjointly down my cheeks, and the squelching noise that accompanies my every footstep arises indistinguishably from the turf and from the inside of my boots. Often on such a day I hear subterranean torrents rushing and gurgling far below, and I feel in my elation that I would like to be carried away by one of them, deep into the gloriously uncomfortable substance of Wales, like riding a dromedary tatterdemalion into Paradise.

In the days of legend travellers returning from such a Welsh escapade were liable to find that they had been away for fifty years and had been written off for dead – everything at home had theatrically changed, young people were old and villages had become cities. I have some of the same sensations when, stripping off my all but liquid clothes and stepping into a steaming bath with the radio on and a book to read, I feel that I truly have passed from one world to another. Actually, of course, I am merely experiencing the true pleasure of masochism – the delight you get when it's all over.

Perhaps the purest, psychotic form of masochism really is a pleasure in suffering. I myself have always been happily susceptible to melancholy and pathos, both aspects of sadness I suppose – contrary to general opinion, I believe that being sorry for someone is the firmest possible foundation for love. Usually, though, what is called masochism is merely the anticipation of relief. He was not a lunatic at all who said, in the old anecdote, that he was banging his head against the wall because it was so nice when he left off – anyone who shells each prawn on the plate before eating a single one is behaving just the same. The only point of hell is its eternity. Even the worst of misfortunes can sometimes give pleasure in retrospect, when all is safely over, while conversely even the greatest pleasures are heightened by the knowledge that they must one day end.

Dreams can offer masochistic pleasures of a kind. One of my own perverser recreations is this: to wake from some horrible dream, find it to be no more than a dream after all, and deliberately recall in the snug comfort of my bed my arraignment before the Gestapo chief, my total inability to remember where I had parked my car, the imminent construction of the new motorway immediately outside my house, my arrival at Heathrow just as the departure of my vital flight was announced, or any other of the recurrent grim experiences that haunt my sleep. Sucks to you, you infantile moron, I say to the Gestapo man then, and I look out of my window with new satisfaction upon the rutted lane which never will, at least until my next nightmare, be turned into a six-lane highway.

Sometimes I tantalize myself with a dangerous extension of this indulgence. I half-persuade myself, when I am wide awake, that I am actually dreaming, and that when I wake up I shall find myself in the middle of some appalling experience, in prison perhaps, or in a hospital ward, or living as a slave in medieval Algiers. The attraction of this perhaps *over*-astringent exercise is the comfort I get from knowing that I have invented it all; the danger lies in the possibility that it is true. ('Perchance to dream', wrote Shakespeare about death's oblivion in the most terrible of all his lines, blithely adopted by Ivor Novello as the title of a frothy musical comedy. 'Ay, there's the rub . . .')

I dreamed a sufficiently astringent poem once, writing it down the moment I woke up, and here it is:

> I haven't seen an antelope
> Since Sunday afternoon.
> I do most anxiously hope
> I see another soon.
>
>
> But if there are no quadrupeds
> To satisfy my whim,
> Tell the man with seven heads
> That I'll make do with him.

By their nature the bitter pleasures are more perilous than others. If they are less likely to give you indigestion, they are more likely to give you colds or lead to heat-exhaustion, and far more likely to induce that sourest of indulgences, cynicism.

So for myself, fond as I am of goats, odd numbers, Welsh rain and bad dreams in retrospect, I try to keep astringency in check (and in prose at least I certainly succeed). William Butler, who thought, incidentally, that the aim of a literary style should be to attract as little attention as possible, was walking through London Zoo one day when he saw two small girls looking at a sleeping hippopotamus. Said one to the other, 'That bird's dead' – and for me the proper limits of astringency are defined within the tale. No bird was dead. The children didn't care anyway. The writer went on his way amused. But when the hippopotamus woke up, it found itself in jail.

21
A Room on a River

Not counting the room I am writing in today, the room that has meant most to me in life is, I am glad to say, one that no longer exists. I would hate to think of other people using it now, fouling it with tobacco smoke or debasing it with trendy furniture. I want my rooms to be always Me, or Us anyway, so I am pleased to know that this particular chamber saved itself from alien tastes by sinking to the bottom of the River Nile.

To get to it from the centre of Cairo you took the big Kasr-el-Nil bridge to the suburb-island of El Gezira, and crossing to the other side, where the western branch of the river flows, walked down an avenue of luscious bougainvillea, purple against the almost invariably cloudless sky. Beneath a trellised gateway, over a gang-plank, and you found yourself upon the deck of a superannuated steamboat, alleged by some romantics to have taken part, long before, in Kitchener's campaign to revenge the death of Gordon. It was now permanently moored beside the river-bank but was still ineffably nautical – tall raked funnel amidships, engines shrouded down below, awnings everywhere against the sun and wheelhouse high above. It had a galley and a saloon, like any proper steamboat; it had state-rooms and deck cabins and a big shady poop; and well forward on its upper deck, square, windowed all round, white-painted but a little blistered by the heat, in the days when I commanded the retired paddle-steamer *Saphir*, in the early 1950s, stood my work-room – the most glamorous room, the most suggestive and the most unforgettable that I have ever occupied.

I was a newspaper correspondent then, covering the Middle East from this unconventional headquarters in Egypt, and my cabin up there above the river was essentially functional. It had no space for frills, because as the former wheel-house it was walled largely in glass. Also I had crammed it with the usual paraphernalia of the foreign correspondent's calling, the maps and telephones and type-writers and piles of official handouts and stacks of newspapers and service cables from head office – pinned to the wall if laudatory, crumpled under the table if not.

But I never thought of it as an office. It was far more than that. Such wall space as it offered sustained the small hopeful library of my youth – the couple of hundred volumes which represented, so to speak, the state of my mind so far. The record-player beside the door (radiogram, as we called it then) was almost always playing Mozart. And there seeped perpetually through its windows an intoxicating assortment of sensual stimuli.

There was the dry dazzling light of Egyptian sunshine. There were the rippling reflections, on my white ceiling, of the majestic river outside. There were exotic smells, of cooking oil, of wood fires, of earthy water, of gasoline. Best of all there were sounds, wonderful sounds – the ruffled roar and hooting of the city streets of course, but also the creaking of timbers, the banging of copper pots and pans, the chanting of the blind Koran singer who sat all day on his wicker chair along the road, and three times a day the call to prayer from the mosque across the river, eddying hauntingly over the water and through the trees, and answered as in echo from countless minarets near and far across the capital.

All around me the life of the river proceeded, intimately near, so that as I sat there among my books I felt truly a part of it. Huge, brownish, deep in the water the feluccas came lurching down-stream, or urgently tacking up, so close that I could hear the grunts and phlegmatic coughing of their crews, and sometimes looked up to see a prickly face grinning back at me through my window only a few feet away. When some especially heavy cargo was being poled upstream the sailors might break into a sonorous river-song, and hour after hour I would hear it, slow and lugubrious, over and over again, fainter and fainter as they heaved their way towards the Equator.

Then there was the presence of the other houseboats moored

along the bank. This was mostly raffish. Plain-clothes policemen paid frequent visits to our neighbourhood, and agreeable suggestions of low life often reached me in my room – high prurient laughter, sudden screams or shoutings, splashes that I took to be the jettisoning of incriminating evidence, all diffused in the general sense of live-and-let-live which, especially in the glorious dog-hours of the Egyptian afternoon, also ruled the responses of my room on the upper deck.

Our own shipboard life proceeded leisurely enough. Often and again my steward Abdu would appear at the open door of my room with a silver coffee-pot upon a silver tray, a jug of buffalo milk and a plate of Playbox biscuits. Now and then the cook shambled by, returning to his quarters after a hubble-bubble of hashish in the privacy of the rope-locker. Slowly, purposefully, methodically about his business went Idris the deck-hand, an aged sailor in a long brown galabiyah topped in cold weather by a blue maritime jersey. His task it was, at the end of a long riverine career, to keep the old steamer afloat and shipshape – rolling and unrolling the awnings, touching up the paintwork, and most important of all, shifting our moorings according to the seasonal rise and fall of the water, which sometimes raised my room high above the street and its trees, and sometimes left us cowering in the lee of the bank.

Idris often sloped past the windows of my room, but somehow he seldom caught my eye. He moved with a preoccupied air, as though he resented what had happened to the ship, forever tied up there, its paddles never to churn again, its engines always silent.

It saddened me, too. I thought it an unworthy fate for the little vessel, even if in fact it had never run the gauntlet of the cataracts with Lord Kitchener; and I was not at all unhappy when, returning to Cairo many years later, and finding only an empty space at our mooring beneath the bougainvillea, I was told the *Saphir* had sunk. Idris, Abdu and the half-stoned cook had gone elsewhere, and only the trellised gateway remained to show where my ship had lain – that and a snatch of Mozart, I fancied, still drifting blithe but wistful across the muddy water.

22
Chaunrikharka

All of us know places – aspects of places even – whose memory can trigger in us haunting sensations of happiness, sadness or plain nostalgia. For me their epitome is Chaunrikharka, which is a speckle of small huts, encouched in gardens and potato fields, somewhere in the Himalayan foothills of East Nepal. I can find it on no map, and it appears in none of the travellers' tales because it is not on the way to anywhere in particular, contains nothing very startling, and is inhabited only by quiet Sherpa hill-people of no particular anthropological allure. Yet the very name of the place, so exotic, so mellifluous on the tongue and so devilishly hard to spell, for thirty-six years has summoned up in me a mood of lyrical and slightly mystical serenity.

I was ill when I went there. Trekking down from Namche Bazar in the company of a Sherpa named Sonam, I was suddenly felled by a combination, I suppose, of fatigue, excitement, altitude sickness and a somewhat cavalier attitude to hygiene. Sonam immediately invited me to spend a few days in his own home. It was only a few miles off the way, he said, and he and his family would see me through my fever.

All Sherpa houses are (or were then) dark, smoky and a little mysterious, except when the inhabitants are in one of their frequently boisterous moods, but Sonam's house in my recollection was darker, smokier and more mysterious than most. This is perhaps because he rolled out my sleeping bag for me in the room which was also the family temple, with a dozen small images of the Buddha, attended by butter-candles, gleaming at the other end. The room was dark, warm, woody, creaky, smoke-blackened, and through its shadows I could always see those gently smiling images, flickered by their candle-light.

Outside the house everything *steamed*. The monsoon was upon us. The rains fell heavily for several hours each day, and the gardens that surrounded Chaunrikharka's six or seven houses were all lush and vaporous. My room had no window, but the open door looked out upon the Sonam family plot, and from it there came a fragrance so profoundly blended of the fertile and the rotten, the sweet and the bitter, the emanations of riotous growth and the intimations of inevitable decay, that still if ever my mind wanders to more sententious subjects I tend to smell the vegetable gardens of Chaunrikharka.

The taste of the potatoes, too, roasted at the family hearth, seemed to me almost philosophically nourishing, while the comfort of the powerful white liquor, *rakhsi*, with which the Sonams now and then dosed me, and the merry voices of the children, frequently hushed lest they disturb my convalescence, and the kind wondering faces of the neighbours who occasionally looked through the open door, and the clatter of the rain on the roof and the hiss of it in the leaves outside, and the enigmatic smiles of those small golden figures in their half-light at the end of the room – all built up in my mind an impression not just of peace and piquancy, but of holiness.

Mind you, it is all a blur to me. Not only have three decades passed since then, but during all my time in Sonam's house I was in a baffled state of mind. This is partly because I was sick, but partly because I did not know then, as I do not know now, precisely where Chaunrikharka was. It seemed in my fancy to be somewhere altogether alone in that wide and marvellous wilderness. One of the great Himalayan peaks rose to the north of us, white as Heaven itself, but I never knew which. A little river rushed through the gully below the house, rocky and slate-grey, but I have no idea what its name was, or where it was going. When we left to resume our march to Katmandu Sonam took me, still in a kind of daze, back to the wide trading track which led from the Sherpa country to the central valley of Nepal, but whether we had been to east or west of it, north or south, I was never entirely sure. Chaunrikharka

might have been an invented place, dreamed up by kindly necro-
mancers to restore me.

Was it? Have I invented it myself? Not, I promise you, in the
fact. Chaunrikharka exists all right, somewhere out there, and I
really did go there with Sonam long ago. But as to what the place
has come to mean to me down the years, that's another matter.
Every place, like every experience, is both active and passive. It
gives to you, and you also give to it, so that its meaning is specific to
you alone. Others might have found in Chaunrikharka stimulants,
depressants perhaps, of altogether different kinds; it is out of my
sensibility that my own image of it comes – my need to match its
fulfilment, my distress to fit its solace, my sickness to find its cure
in that quiet darkened room. So it is that I carry my Chaunrikharka
wherever I go, frequently sensing the hot steamy damp of its fields
as I lean from my window at home, and remembering the silent
Buddhas among their candles, when the softer rain of Gwynedd
spatters my roof.

23
Russian Ambiguities

Foreigners who went to Moscow in the 1960s were likely to meet the renegade British diplomat Guy Burgess. Whether on the instructions of the KGB, or because of his own nostalgia, he often got in touch with visiting actors and actresses, journalists and authors – the sort of people, I suppose, least likely to rebuff him. He very soon contacted me when I arrived in the city in 1960 to report the trial of the American pilot, Gary Powers, whose spy plane had been shot down over Siberia. In those days visiting newspaper people were carefully tagged by the authorities – I remember well how immediately, when I introduced some speculation about the trial into a private conversation, the cold voice of an unknown censor cut me off – and it was not long before Burgess came to call on me at the Metropole Hotel.

We had champagne and caviare (so cheap then that I virtually lived on it, as if it were bread and cheese) and he confided in me, as he confided in everyone, his lingering affection for England, his concern for his mother, the hope that one day the British Government might allow him to go home for a visit. As he well knew, if he had so much as set foot on British soil the British Government would have strung him up as a traitor, but disbelieving myself in the crime of treason – we have a right, in my view, to choose our own loyalties – I could not help being sorry for the poor wretch, whose Foreign Office elegance was by then running to fat, whose manners had become a little gross, but whose humour was still entertaining. We accordingly agreed to go together that evening to the Bolshoi, for which I had a couple of tickets, and arranged to meet outside the theatre door.

When I got there he was waiting on the steps. I waved a greeting as I approached him through the crowd, but by the time I had reached the door he had vanished. I never saw him again. Was he required for other duties after all? Was the appointment considered unsuitable? Was it all caprice? I shall never know; nor can I remember now, so many years later, whether it was on that evening or another when, ushered alone into a Bolshoi box for the inevitable *Swan Lake*, I found the bulky form of a plain-clothes policeman posted in the shadows behind me, and Mr and Mrs Nikita Khrushchev, with guests from Africa, larger than life in the very next box.

I was raised on Russia – or rather, on Constance Garnett's Russia, having inherited my grandfather's probably ignorant preference for her translations of the Russian writers. Sometimes nowadays I look forward with delight to a world – my children's world perhaps – in which the Soviet Union will be as open and familiar to us all as the United States. At other times I feel that Earth will be a less interesting planet without the Russian enigma, as it has been made much duller, I think, by man's reaching the moon, and would be made duller still if they ever solved the problem of the Loch Ness Monster. For better or for worse, the strangeness of Russian life that Constance Garnett first revealed to me, its peculiar blend of the earthy and the esoteric, has bewitched me ever since.

Time and again some projection of Russia into our more ordinary world has fuelled the enchantment for me. One day in the 1950s, for instance, when the Soviet Union was just beginning to exhibit to the world at large its diplomatic as against its subversive skills, I was at Cairo Airport when the Soviet Foreign Minister of the day, the now utterly forgotten Dmitri Shepilov, arrived on an official mission to the Egyptians. Egypt was ruled by soldiers then, and a group of officers walked out to the tarmac to meet their distinguished guest. They looked nervous and fulsome, fingering their epaulettes, tidying their medals; and when the aircraft door opened, and Shepilov appeared at the top of the steps, they looked up at him as if he had come from another planet. He was a big pudgy man, extremely pale, as if he had never sat in the sunshine ever; and shambling down the steps towards the salutes and outstretched hands of the Egyptians, while a band played the *Red Flag* as though it were sight-reading the piece, he seemed to me to

123

bring with him all the colossal tedium of secrecy, size and timeless-
ness that I thought of as Mother Russia.

In a minor way I get the same ambivalent excitement from the
sight of a stocky Lada saloon, mule-like among the Fords and Fiats
of a Welsh country road. In a major way I got it when, boarding
an aircraft in Geneva one day, I saw advancing down a runway the
immense, multi-wheeled, droop-winged, swollen grey behemoth of
an aircraft which was really bringing Mr Gorbachev's bullet-proof
limousines to a summit conference, but which might just as well
have been full of bortsch. I feel it when I see the red flag and
Cyrillic script on a freighter somewhere, with its fat red-faced
women leaning over its rail telling each other, I imagine, obscene
anecdotes of Georgia. And far away I certainly felt the old thrill,
part dread, part fascination, when I went searching for the writer
Alexander Solzhenitsyn in his exile in Vermont. I never met him,
but that hardly mattered in the end – just finding his house in the
woods was frisson enough.

The woods were far thicker than I expected, and the silence of
the place was a great deal more silent. Somehow it seemed later
in the evening than I had planned. Tall metal gates, with television
cameras, floodlights, a bell-button and a microphone, barred the
entrance to Solzhenitsyn's retreat, and beyond them a long dark
drive disappeared into the woods towards the homestead out of
sight. When I switched off the engine and got out of the car the
silence was absolute but for the distant wild barking of dogs, far
away among the trees in the gathering dark. I looked at that gate,
I listened to those dogs, I eyed that camera, I stood alone in that
dark silence; and so it was that I never did meet the writer, but
instead have preserved, from that moment to this, an indelible
sense of Russia's ambiguities, expressed on the other side of the
world among the genial New England woods.

Ample Mrs Khrushchev smiled a greeting at me at the Bolshoi:
the KGB man sighed audibly at moving moments of the performance, and once touched me on the shoulder to share his emotion.
Mixed in my mind with the queerness of Russia has been its extra
concentration of humanity, all the more beguiling because it is
unexpected. In Mauritius long ago I found myself driving along a

road behind a truck-load of Russian sailors – they were from the cruiser *Sverdlov*, and had come to the island to help clear up the aftermath of a hurricane. They looked tired, slumped all over the place in the back of the truck, fine big men with their caps tilted over their eyes or pushed to the backs of their heads. I gave them a wave, if only to thank them for what they were doing, and their responses were touching. They had been told by the shipboard commissars, I imagine, to have no contact with westerners ashore, so it was only after long thought, after exchanging speculative glances with one another, and a few words, after slightly tidying themselves up, straightening their caps, pulling their shoulders back, that with shy smiles a few of them ventured to return my greeting as I put my foot down and overtook them.

Once a colleague and I wanted to attend the Moscow lying-in-state of some Soviet Academician, I forget who, because rumour suggested that he was not dead at all, but had been sent into permanent exile. A close cordon of troops surrounded the building in which his corpse was supposed to lie, inspecting everyone's passes. We had no passes, and two or three soldiers of elemental aspect barred our way, fur-capped and heavily armed. On the spur of the moment I produced an invitation card to a diplomatic cocktail party, which I happened to have with me. They examined the card very attentively the right way up, passing it between each other with heavy frowns and mutterings. They turned it upside down, looked at the back of it, held it up to the light and felt its texture. Finally, with an abandon that was Russian all over, they gave up, shrugged their shoulders, burst into laughter, all but tossed the card in the air and broke ranks to admit us to the presence of the Academician (who, if it really was him, looked very dead indeed).

'What's this?' demanded a Leningrad customs official curtly one day, extracting a typescript from my baggage, and simultaneously eyeing my then epicene figure. 'It's a psychological novel,' said I. 'Ah, a psychological novel,' he replied in a voice of infinite understanding, as though I had shared a confidence with him; and carefully repacking the script in my suitcase, waved me through.

'We have nothing against Lenin, nothing at all,' I remember a British Ambassador in Moscow telling me, rather as though he were battling with his conscience. It is hard to imagine anyone actually preferring life in the Soviet Union to life in the west, but the magic of theoretical Communism, allied with the allure of Russia itself, is powerful stuff indeed, and I am not in the least surprised that between the world wars so many fine minds in the west were seduced by it. That they were not equally repelled by the horrible excesses of Stalinism seems to me one of Russia's own mysteries, passed on by auto-suggestion to spellbound intellects elsewhere.

I have always been attracted to the idea of Communism, and still think that if it could be made a system of happiness rather than mere welfare, it might overcome the world. Not being of the right age, however, I cannot tell whether I too would have suc-cumbed to the call of Soviet Communism in the 1930s. The war spared my generation that quandary, and by the time it was over it was plain to see that Bolshevism had failed its prophets and disciples, and betrayed both the Communist ideal and the Soviet revolution. I first came face to face with the Russians in Vienna, when Austria was jointly occupied by the western and eastern allies, and their stony demeanours and baleful activities certainly did not make me feel that I was born to the wrong side of any ideological fence.

Who indeed could really suppose, I used to wonder in the years after the war, that the drab dogmatic mufflement of eastern Europe could represent any liberation of mankind? Russia was patently leading its puppets and surrogates in the wrong direction. I was never in the least surprised that Communism failed abjectly to recruit the ex-colonial nations, as they were released from their respective Empires, and never for a moment did I suppose that the ramshackle Soviet State, with its dingy standards, its outdated convictions, its discredited values, its corruptions and its leadership by fusty old men of fusty views, could represent any true threat to the glittering stimulants of capitalism. The vast majority of the inhabitants of this world, I long ago came to appreciate, would really like to be American; precious few, given the choice, would plump for Soviet citizenship.

Yet even in those dreary Cold War years, the years of Beria and Khrushchev and Brezhnev and Andropov, Russia never ceased to beguile me. I was at the General Assembly of the United Nations in 1962 when, in a famous incident, Khrushchev took off his shoe and banged it on his table in protest during a speech by the British Prime Minister, Harold Macmillan. Macmillan, twitching his mouth to bare his teeth in the dog-like grimace that served him for a smile, asked the President of the Assembly for a translation, a sally which was hailed by his admirers as a masterly demonstration of sang-froid, but was I suspect simply the first thing that came into his head. Khrushchev anyway, grinning, shouting and nodding his bald head, continued to hit the table with his shoe until, with much commotion, order was restored to the chamber.

Just what it was about, history and I have probably both forgotten. I was sitting in the Waldorf-Astoria bar later that evening when Macmillan came shuffling elegantly through, baring his teeth right and left. The Americans rose to applaud him as he passed, as if to congratulate him upon his gentlemanly rebuff of a loutish opponent. I was not however quite so sure. It seemed to me that there had been a peasant honesty and humour to Khrushchev's gesture which a more sensitive man than Macmillan might well have exploited. The graceless form of the Russian, banging away there, stuck in my mind not so much as the image of a boorish dictator, but as a kind of folk-figure, a character from a Russian story-book. Though I expect whatever argument he was supporting was specious, I felt myself obscurely on his side; and I have since learnt, as a matter of fact, that the gesture of banging one's shoe on the table, to express disagreement, is no more than an Old Russian Custom.

I like to imagine – one always does – that were I a Russian myself I would have fought bravely, through the worst days of Soviet oppression, for openness and liberty. Surely everyone's patience must sometimes crack, faced with the very vastness of Russia, its monotony of system as of landscape. In Odessa once, finding my hotel bedroom unacceptably hot, I took up a shoe like Khrushchev and broke one of its impenetrably sealed windows. This is something I would not have done anywhere else in the world, and I was induced to do it, I suspect, partly because I knew the hotel to be the property of the all-enveloping State, but more interestingly, because it was in Odessa alone, of all Soviet cities, that I ever felt myself to be followed. Perhaps the irritating presence of that sauntering figure behind me, wherever I went, goaded me into this foolish act of independence (foolish, because the Odessans know their climate better than I do, and by morning I was frozen stiff).

Will something be lost, if ever Russia becomes truly free, and spirits are not fired to these passions by the deadweight of the Establishment? Certainly the characters of its literature, like the characters of its recent art and politics, are so compelling because they act out their lives in the shadow of authority; they are always, whether in the pages of the old novelists or on the television news, defying decrees or official tradition, hiding from the secret police, arranging protest meetings, experimenting with forbidden foreign ideas, being sent to Siberia, fleeing to Switzerland, having their stories censored, joining the army or saying prayers for the Holy Czar. I find it hard to imagine the Russian genius without this gigantic superstructure of received system, just as I find it difficult even now to conceive a Moscow ablaze with neon advertisements, alive with Saabs or Renaults, with a McDonald's around the corner from Red Square and soft porn magazines at the new kiosks – in short, in the condition of any normal capital city, almost anywhere else in the developed world.

Do I wish it so? Of course. A superb country, creative almost beyond our imagination, may emerge from the emancipation of the Soviet Union. Apart from those who have fought so heroically for individual rights, millions of citizens may discover a kind of fulfilment they can hardly dream of, while the rest of us, everywhere in the world, may find for ourselves comrades we hardly know, experiences marvellously fresh and exciting. And yet . . . Perversely, sentimentally really, it is partly the arcane despotism of Russia that compels me so. It is wrong, but it is true, and even as I admit it I apologize to all those poor souls who have suffered in prison or labour camp precisely because of that very abstraction. Sometimes in Stockholm, a bastion of all things free, fair, comfortable and logical, one sees in the evening a Soviet liner sailing off to Leningrad. The lights of the kindly city are coming on, its well-fed burghers are promenading the quayside, and from its buildings emanate suggestions of warm and easy pleasures to come; but when I see that ship go by, Hammer and Sickle at the stern, part of my heart goes apprehensively with it, to its dark and marvellous destination in the east.

24
A Week of Escape

Once, at a frenzied moment of life, I had a week in Ootacamund, 'The Queen of Indian Hill Station', which the British Empire created for itself in the Nilgiri Hills south of Mysore. I did not go there on any post-imperial nostalgia trip. I went because all I had read about modern Ooty (as the place is universally known, even on timetables) encouraged me to think that I might find there, so long after the departure of the Raj, a last stronghold of the temperate bourgeois values – just what I wanted, I thought, to get my breath back. For don't we all, from time to time, pine for those conventional certainties, those comfortable rules of decorum and restraint, that our grandparents are alleged to have enjoyed?

Certainly the road signs seemed encouraging, as we drove up the twisting forest road from Mettupalayam, feeling cooler and kinder with each passing mile, now and then swerving to avoid heedless troops of monkeys, and honking with resonant effect at horseshoe bends. MAKE NO HASTE, the hoardings said. DRIVE SAFE. AVOID OVER-SPEEDING. LIFE IS MORE VALUABLE THAN TIME.

Much more valuable. For my first couple of days in Ooty I did not leave the grounds of the Savoy Hotel, which started its career as a mission school in the nineteenth century. Nothing could be more genteely restorative than this dear old place, or more evocative of less demanding times. Almost on tiptoe the bearer brought my morning tea, properly cosied of course, to the flowered garden rooms around the back, where the only sounds were the occasional scufflings of rats or night-birds above the ceiling, and the comfortable gurglings of the Elephant Pattern cistern in the bathroom. At one o'clock I ate my chicken sandwiches and drank my gin-and-lime (Permit Number 457843) in the shadow of the great gum-tree on the lawn, surrounded by homely phlox and wallflower, and scarcely disturbed by the efforts of the Old British Resident to get the BBC news on his neighbouring verandah.

Dinner-time found me over my curry and stewed fruit among the wood-panels and serried willow-patterns of the Dining Hall, where a log fire danced aromatically beneath the florid mantlepiece, and all around me miraculously well-behaved Indian families asked for the chupattis, please, in ever-considerate undertones. And when bed-time came, and I shuffled through the dim lights back to Room 9, in her wicker chair in the gloaming I would find the *ayah* of the family next door, on watch outside their bungalow to see the baby went to sleep. 'Goodnight *ayah*,' I would say, as to the manner born, and 'Goodnight, Auntie,' she habitually replied.

So far, so good. It truly was an ordered little world of its own, and I spent most of my time, very properly I thought, drawing pictures in the garden. Scents of blossom and eucalyptus attended me there, and ever and again with a skid of hoofs on gravel the hotel ponies scampered into sight from the back of the house, small children clamped in grim delight upon their saddles, grooms in trilby hats and buttoned suits breathlessly behind.

Outside our hedges Ooty gently stirred, and muffled sounds of Indian life impinged: the crowing of cocks, the barking of dogs, the cawing of queer rooks like yelping hounds, a beat of drums sometimes from the bazaar, a whistle-hoot from the railway station. Dimly beyond the garden, too, Ooty shapes revealed themselves. Gabled villas were half-hidden in thickets, and the skyline above them was jagged with tall stands of wattle or acacia. Here and there patches of bare grassland showed, and invariably across them, whenever I chanced to look, two or three women in vivid saris were elegantly toiling. Cows wandered in and out of my vision. Sometimes a flock of goats dawdled superciliously by.

One afternoon there was a powerful rainstorm, and I retired for tea and biscuits to my room. When the rain stopped and I returned to the garden, all its scents were twice as strong, all its sounds were magnified in the moist air, and the slopes and ridges of the Nilgiris stretched away clear and glistening in the evening sun, as though a brand new country had been created out there in my absence.

On the third day I broke the garden bounds, and entered that landscape myself. Oddly enough Ooty seemed smaller outside than it did from within the compound. Physically it is scattered widely enough over its hillsides, but socially it is very concentrated. Eyes are on you always, eyes from Shinkow's Chinese Restaurant or the officers' Holiday Home, eyes between the chinks of bungalow blinds or through the topiary of the municipal garden, so that long before you have reached Charing Cross and turned into the newsagents to buy your paper, people down there have known you to be on your way. 'Staying at the Savoy, I believe?' says a shop-keeper you have never before set eyes on. 'We will present ourselves at your Room No 9 this evening,' threatens the official with a winsome smile, 'to introduce ourselves properly, and make your good self welcome.'

It is a grim and tidy town, as Indian towns go, and wandering through it is like inspecting a civic exhibition. Small boats are paddled decorously across the municipal lake. The train from Mettupalayam puffs indefatigably into its ornamented station. Horses career like clockwork round the little racecourse, losing me 50 rupees on Mr Rajagoplan's Magic Flash, but perfectly complementing the *amour-propre* of the Madras Race Club members posed like actors and actresses in their grandstand. There are pasteboard-style palaces here and there, built for the recreation of Maharajahs, and homely old villas with names like The Cedars or Tudor Hall. Even the bazaar operates on a recognizably reduced scale of oriental intensity.

All this was just what I required. What perfection of the middle-class ideal, I thought, those neat trellised bungalows behind their protective hedges, decorated with bargeboard and touches of half-timbering, roofed often enough in rustic tiling and surmounted by impressive chimney-clumps! How aloof to time and anxiety, those tranquil lawns beneath their towering trees, those tidy rows of geranium-pots, those white gates and bowered porches!

Often I was invited in, and given tea or lemonade. The family of a Bombay businessman showed me their holiday villa at the top end of town, where the gardener looked up discreetly to observe my reaction to the herbaceous border, and Sir Frederick Price's gigantic *History of Ootacamund* lay open on the drawing-room table. The secretary of the Ooty Club urged me to make myself at home in the apparently permanently deserted splendour of its rooms, where slaughtered jackals and slaughtering Masters of the Hunt are reconciled at last upon the walls, and the bar looks as though nobody has ordered a Scotch for half a century. I was given the run of the Nilgiri Library, with its covetable collection of Victorian books still hopefully awaiting, it seemed to me, a few Victorian readers, and on the Sunday morning I was ushered hospitably to a pew in St Stephen's Church (named not so much for the Proto-martyr as for the late Mr Stephen Lushington, Indian Civil Service).

Exactly the pleasures I wanted of Ootacamund: calm, amusing, courteous, *respectable* pleasures.

Yet in the end a trace of disillusion set in, and made my week in Ooty a wistful kind of refreshment after all. During my final days I extended my range again, and inviting Mr V. M. Krishna (Door No 40, Church Hill Road, behind the Coronation Talkies) to accommodate me in his hired car, drove out of town. The original point of Ooty was its setting, 7,500 feet up, in a landscape which generations of travellers likened to England. It reminded Edward Lear of Leatherhead. It thrilled Lord Lytton with 'such beautiful *English* rain, such delicious *English* mud'. 'I expect you feel perfectly at home here,' every Ooty hostess tells a visitor from Britain, 'everyone says it's just like Sussex.'

But I realized, as I pottered around with Mr Krishna, that it had never been really like Sussex: only like a vague image of Sussex, conceived by people who had been too long away from home. It was a substitute landscape for the exiled British, a place they wished for, and it is upon similar bitter-sweet self-delusions that the Queen of Hill Stations subsists today. Charming it is in its allusions, fresh and wholesome by comparison, but it is only an old pretence, passed on by a sort of historical osmosis from the

133

lost Empire to its successors. So I was not altogether sorry when
my week came to an end, and I returned to the struggle.

25
Australian Distractions

I was sitting recently upon a grassy incline in a park in Adelaide, South Australia, when two small boys, one rather smaller than the other, prepared to ride down the slope on their skateboards. There were a few beer-bottles lying around, left over from the night before, and I heard the elder boy say to the younger, in an authoritative voice intended largely for my own ears: 'Please don't hit the lady – I don't mind about the beer bottles, but *definitely* not the lady.'

They were splendidly entertaining children, and they brought to a head feelings about Australia which I had been working on and worrying about for years. They were free, it seemed to me, of all inherited regret, shame, cringe or pretension. They did not give a damn whether they were or were not descended from convicts. Their racial origins seemed to be mixed – a touch of Greek, perhaps, or Lebanese? – and they certainly knew of no Mother Country but their own. They were a couple of clean sheets, and upon their personalities, I surmised as I watched them fooling about, history and geography were about to write new messages.

In 1780 the Frenchman Michel-Guillaume de Crèvecoeur introduced his readers to 'the American, this new man'. Since his time we have not really had another addition to our species, but perhaps, I thought in the park that day, one is coming up.

My first landfall in Australia was at Darwin, Northern Territory, nearfly forty years ago. I had decided to jump into Australia at the deep end, and spend a week or two exploring that then benighted coast. The town was dismal in the extreme, so dismal that it has left in my memory only a blur of brick and corrugated iron, and the hotel was just as depressing: an unlovely pub-like hostelry whose dinner-table I was obliged to share, feeling extraordinarily effete and fastidious, with half a dozen homespun sons of the south. What was I then, they asked me, a rich travelling Pom come to look at the other hall? 'I am a sort of a writer,' I replied with dignity. A sort of a writer! That's the truth! A sort of a writer, and they knew what sort, they'd met that sort before!

Having got through these preliminaries, conventional in the Australia of the time, we grew quite friendly, and in the end I rather enjoyed Darwin – since utterly transformed, incidentally, by a combination of hurricane and tourist trade. Nevertheless on the whole the Australia of the early 1960s was not for me. It was an extremely self-conscious country, exaggeratedly independent in some ways, preposterously sycophantic in others. Its history still split it, so to speak, into jailers and convicts – the jailers ridiculously British, monarchist, racist and snobby, the convicts contumaciously Irish in spirit if not in blood. They were united only by a common sense of social and patriotic insecurity: as an Australian novelist would put it to me much later, tugging a forelock and saying 'Fuck you!' both at the same time. Cricket, royalty, booze, beaches, the Great War, the ideal of working-class fraternity they called 'mateship', these were the national enthusiasms, and they were supplemented by crude displays of male chauvinism, ethnic prejudice and Philistinism.

It was no place for a writer of my work. When I wrote an essay about Sydney it was five full years before the last letter of complaint reached me from down under.

Look at Sydney now! No city on earth so enlivens me, the moment I set foot in it, with a sense of fresh start. It is one of the most endemically corrupt municipalities in the western world, dominated by millionaires of frightful rapacity, but this only enhances its sense of inexhaustible opportunity. I love to walk around its central waterfront on a bright summer morning, say. People are very open and natural then – the joggers smile breathless smiles, the early park workers pause for a chat, layabouts summon a phrase or two of badinage and the first commuters, disembarking from the ferries at Circular Quay, still have time for greetings. Above the scene looms the harbour bridge, a very British, very 1930-ish, very George V-like, very male, very strong, graceless and orthodox thing. When I first went to Sydney that bridge was the unchallenged symbol of the place. Now it seems almost incongruous, the waterfront's one surviving reminder of the old colonial Australia. Otherwise, it appears to me nowadays as I take my exercise towards Wooloomolloo, everything around me proclaims Sydney to be entirely self-created.

Certainly no outsider could have invented its climate, its foliage or its terrain, all of which still somehow give me the impression that Australia really is upside-down, as we used to think in childhood. Australian water does in fact go down the drain the other way round, and much else about the nature of things seems to me reversed, or at best confused. The trees seem to grow wrong, and bear the wrong sorts of leaf. The birds fly with weird flapping motions and make unknown cries. That lovely harbour, with its steep banks and myriad inlets, always suggests to me a fjord in a continent of ice, the sort of place Atlantic expeditions winter their ships in, except that it has miraculously sprouted green woods and gardens. Above all there is something queer about the light. It is a northern, Scandinavian light, but reversed – just as the black swan of Australia is like a northern swan in negative. Where it should be moist, it is dry; where it should be pale, it is golden; and when, a cloud coming up from the south, it looks as though we ought to be expecting a snow-shower, nothing but a passing shadow momentarily darkens the scene.

Such are the primeval pleasures I get these days during my morning exercise in Sydney, but superimposed on them are pleasures of extreme modernity. The new buildings of the city glitter and strut. Hydrofoils sweep superbly, with curves of foam, away from the quay towards Manly and the beaches. I imagine a mesh of electronic beams, rays and signals crossing the sky. And presiding over it all nowadays, having displaced on every tourist poster that lumpish bridge, Sydney's Opera House spreads its wings provocatively beside the water – perhaps the most reckless municipal building ever erected anywhere, and not at all unlike, now I come to think of it, some primeval amphibious creature itself.

The elder of the two boys, whizzing down the slope once more, swung around to stop with a glorious flourish at my feet. 'What skill!' he observed with a winning smile.

He did not say it boastfully – ten years old though he was, at the most, he was amused at himself. One of the things I like best about contemporary Australia is its frank and entertained self-admiration. The pride of this country, when it was not chip-on-shoulder, used to be a derivative, second-hand pride, and the capital city of Canberra was designed as a pompous declaration of such sentiments, built to European patterns to represent imported values. The new Parliament Building, however, is exactly the opposite. Built within the mass of a hill, it is an assembly chamber quite properly inside-out; a recognition of the fact that the nature of Australia is almost inconceivably strange, and that its original inhabitants are as close to the earth as the kangaroos and platypuses themselves. Without the aborigines, however sad they are, however misused, Australia would not be half so interesting. The glimpses one has of them almost everywhere in the country, if only sloping hang-dog through city streets, enhance the science-fiction quality of the country, but also give it historical authenticity. They are essential to the national meaning. Their fretful figures are evidence that Australia does have a pedigree of its own, and soon enough, I venture to prophecy, Australians of all sorts will be finding it fashionable to claim aboriginal blood.

The swift absorption too of Greeks, Italians, Lebanese, Germans, even Chinese and Japanese into the national mainstream has released the Australians from manghy of their old hang-ups. I remember years ago being astonished by the spectacle of an Australian man holding in his arms a baby, in those days almost a contradiction in terms. Approaching closer, I realized him to be what they then called a New Australian – not, that was to say, absolutely a proper true-blue, Dinkum Aussie Australian, whose father had fought at Gallipoli and whose great-great-grandparents were either related to the Duke of Newcastle or had been transported to Botany Bay merely for tumbling a squire's daughter in the hay – not, in short, quite the real thing, but an immigrant from continental Europe. Today the New Australians have won the day, socially at least. Their manners and standards are supreme. I would not look twice at a man carrying a baby now, the pubs are no longer quite

138

so grotesquely macho and a vast corpus of nostalgia, based upon Britishness, war and class, has been expunged from the national psyche. Robert Menzies, a particularly resilient Prime Minister of Australia, once told me that whenever he arrived over London, and looked down from his aircraft to see old grime of the place vaporized into black smoke above the capital, he felt a tremor of pride and inherited loyalty. I imagine that few Australians would get such a thrill now, and several millions of them indeed have no connection with the British Isles whatever.

Not long ago I went to an ethnic parade in Melbourne, in which all the different racial groups of the city presented themselves in tableau, float or marching band. It was raining, and the festivities had a slightly muted air, the canopies, feathers and papier mâché of the floats wilting a little in the damp, the more elderly of the marchers looking resolutely rather than spontaneously cheerful. Yet the message was easy to read. Those old people were people like the rest of us, and showed in their faces more or less the same experiences, of climate, of history, of diet, that have moulded the faces of half the world. But their sons, daughters and grandchildren were the New People. Looking down from those lurching floats, dressed up as they were in Greek skirts, Ukrainian caps or Sicilian sabots, their faces of brown and gold sailed through the rain with an air of revelation, like evangelists riding by.

The skateboard boys stopped for a chat. 'At the corner of our road there's a house full of aborigines,' the younger one told me, 'and one day the aborigine lady knocked on our door and her head was all bleeding and now her husband's gone to prison.' 'For a long time?' I inquired. 'For a very, very long time,' he said.

I detected no *schadenfreude* in his reportage – they were kindly children – but all the same the anecdote gave me a jolt, as I lay there in the benign sunshine, and reminded me that Australia without its streak of malice would not be Australia at all. Even there in Adelaide, the most gentlemanly of Australian cities, where never a convict was transported – even in Adelaide a strain of bitterness surfaces. Crime there is often bizarre, as though the impulse to violence has twisted its way out of the national subconscious, and I sometimes think that the Australian gift for malignant abuse springs not from history at all, but is a product of the country's very substance, so bitter, so brooding, so full of grudge. They say the koala bear, that darling star of the Australian fauna, can be a horrid little beast, and a snide comment from the Australian Press, which is one of the most mischievous in the western world, is not unlike a nasty nip from an emu.

It strikes me as essentially a malice of the past, part of the old Australia. When I hear some middle-aged citizen, wearing shorts and long stockings, loudly calling his companion 'Mate', or even 'Cobber', I feel always that this traditional bonhomie, now beginning to seem unnatural or defensive, could easily be soured into ill-will. In a cultural sense you could not, in my experience, entirely trust the Old Australian. It once fell to me, long ago, to propose the toast at the Anzac Day dinner at Oxford. I gave a speech in what was I hoped the true Oxford vein, making the conventional fun of Australian manners, concluding with expressions of admiration which were, as it happened, perfectly true. To my horror I found that the guest delegated to respond to my toast was an Old Australian of the most utterly short-trousered and long-stockinged kind; not indeed the Mate or Cobber kind because he was immensely grand, being at once a General and a Judge of the High Court, but certainly imbued with just the same values. I expected the worst, and got it – not a fancy of mine but was cruelly demolished, hardly a joke but was taken with offence, and all the nice things I had said about Australia were rejected as ignorant or impertinent.

I suppose such old stiffs still stalk the Australian landscape, responding to toasts and rebuffing upstarts, but fortunately I do not meet them. Young people run most aspects of Australian life today, and Australia is one country where the young people are more dignified, more courteous and more sure of themselves than the old.

Perhaps even the innate malevolence will fade with time. In the park that day I observed, sitting on a nearby bench, a couple in late middle age who were clearly British immigrants – I could tell that by their stooped postures and their air of complaint. I would guess they had come to Australia in the 1950s, and had brought with them something of their mean frustrated homeland, where backs were still stooped by the effects of history, and attitudes were soured by social system. As they sat there smoking their cigarettes (ash drooping at the tip), two young mounted constables passed by, one male, one female, both of supernal handsomeness, high on white horses in the sunshine. As they rode past the English couple they smiled down at them dazzling smiles of benevolence; the old people nodded subserviently in reply, dropping ash on their laps.

It was like seeing evolution actually happening – the immigrants so ineradicably rooted in their origins, the passing cops so radiantly of a developing species that I thought they might easily prove, if stripped of their uniforms, actually marsupial. Even in Australia, though, there can be no such thing as an entirely clean break. History cannot be cancelled. Soon afterwards the younger of the two skateboard boys, pausing once again, told me that his father had lately taken part in a military parade. 'What kind of a hat did he wear?' I asked for something to say. One of those hats, he said, which were flat on one side, but turned up on the other. 'I know,' I said, 'like they used to wear in the Great War.'

There was a silence for a moment, and then the boy spoke. 'I *hate* the Great War,' he said: and my heart turned.

26
A Colleague

When I heard one day in the 1970s that David Holden was dead, his body having been found murdered on the road between Cairo airport and the city, it came as a great sadness but not exactly a shock. Our friendship was that of colleagues, and it had been enjoyed always against an esoteric background, a background somewhat romantic and adventurous, and not without a string of intrigue – the background through which foreign correspondents in murkier parts of the world habitually moved. He had succeeded me as Middle East correspondent of *The Times*, and later as roving correspondent of the *Guardian*, and for years our ways crossed frequently and often exotically, in Jordan or in Cuba, Muscat or Rhodesia.

Wherever I went he seemed lately to have been, and vice versa. In Britain he sometimes breezed in upon us unexpected, and when I needed enlivenment I occasionally knocked unannounced upon the door of his house in Islington – if he was not there his wife Ruth might be, and she was just as welcoming. When the fact of my trans-sexualism came to light, patently ending a phase of our acquaintance, or at least putting it on a new footing, he came down to Bath to interview me for the *New York Times*; I kissed him on the cheek when we parted at the railway station, for the sake of auld lang syne.

We exchanged frequent picture postcards, generally expressing ourselves in limericks or snatches of comic verse, and in fact he had posted a card to me on the very morning of his death, before he flew from Amman to Egypt to be shot in the back of the neck.

It was a friendship, for me at least, peculiarly opaque and elusive.

142

We did not know each other intimately, or even very well. We met for the first time in adulthood, and we were very different sorts of people. David was a Geordie, stocky, blue-eyed and compellingly good-looking, who talked a precisely correct English and had been educated partly in America. Though his father was a well-known and highly respected journalist in the North, he had originally thought of being an actor, and there was to him a certain aura of The Player. He stood and moved rather as he might on stage, bearing himself consciously, and his attitude to his profession was not quite that of reporter, but more impresarial, as though he had a managing interest in the events he described. By general consent he was the most brilliant British correspondent of his generation, wise, witty and accurate, but in fact he always seemed to me *hors concours*, approaching the business in a different way from everyone else. He was a lover of gardens, and there was something essentially serene and contemplative to his manner of doing things.

Like an actor he had a taste for the grand gesture, but like a gardener he was in no hurry. He was once in an antique shop in Jerusalem with another correspondent when the two of them saw, both at the same time, an Islamic pottery bowl of exquisite allure. Both wanted it badly, but it was David, having more money in this pocket at that moment, who took it home. Ten years later the colleague found it left to him in David's will. It was as though the immediate was not important to him – as though he worked to a separate calendar perhaps, or had another conception of time. Sometimes he used to present an evening news programme on the BBC in London, and nobody ever did it with such measured pace and deliberation; by the time he reached his professional peak I had left newspapers, but so far as I know he never cared much about scoops or petty deadlines.

This was how David Holden seemed to me, but the portrait may be quite erroneous. I can write about him only in a slight way, because I knew him no more deeply, but I was peculiarly affected by his personality, and am haunted still by the memory of his presence. Ruth rang me once to ask my views about his death. When I ventured to suggest that it might be best to abandon her quest for an explanation she thought, I suspect, that I was conveying

143

some kind of warning, from the intelligence community perhaps; but I meant only that if I were her I would leave his life as it stood, ending in tragic mystery. A certain enigma had surrounded him always, for me anyway, showing itself in those pale blue eyes, that meditative stance, and aesthetically at least it seemed to me right that his story should find no conclusion.

Because the enigma proved, as it were, real. We none of us know to this day why David died. The police in Egypt and in England failed to arrest a murderer, all the legions of investigative journalism failed to find the truth. The terrible conclusion to a charismatic life will probably be dispersed for ever in legend, surmise, half-truth and footnote.

Not that it is any of my business, really. He was only a colleague, and it is an impertinence perhaps even to speculate about a memory that belongs so much more truly to others. I cannot account for the strength of the pull that I always felt between us, like the force of some magnetic field. Perhaps it was partly physical, but it was mostly an airy kind of fascination; and I dare say it was only I who sensed it.

Anyway, I miss him still, and it gives me an ambivalent kind of pleasure when I sometimes think I see him, walking in front of me in a foreign street, or silent in a café. The card he sent me on the day of his death, which showed a view of the Citadel in Jerusalem, bore a message that seemed to me puzzling – not a mere frivolous greeting such as we usually exchanged, but one that tantalizingly seemed to convey something between its lines, if only I could read it. When the news of the murder reached me I had the card sent to Scotland Yard, in case it might afford some clue to the tragedy; but it does not seem to have helped, and I wish they would let me have it back again, for sentimental reasons.

27
To the Mountains

Some time during every day, at my home in Wales, I switch off my word processor, clear my mind of the passage I am writing, and go out for a break. I walk along the seashore, or down the river bank, or across the meadows in front of my house; and sometimes I undertake something different in kind, and climb up our neighbouring mountain. Every culture, I think, sees something holy in mountains, and I am especially susceptible to their numen: two in particular, Arenig Fawr in Wales, Mont Canigou in the south of France, give me tremors of inexplicable and tantalizing excitement whenever I see them – when I go from one to the other, it is though I have been travelling along some arcane line of energy direct from Gwynedd to Roussillon.

Bryn Pentyrch is not in that category. We call all hills mountains in Wales, and this one is only 359 feet high, offering a walk more than a climb really; but it is such a layered kind of place, all the same, and is so instinct with memories and allusions, that although reaching the top takes only half an hour or so, I think of it as an expedition.

In a way the hill is upside-down, for contrary to usual mountain practice the foot of it rather than the summit is its holiest part. A spring emerges from the hillside there, and in medieval times the Celtic saint Cybi set himself up in a hermitage nearby. His well became famous, pilgrims flocked to be cured of their ailments in his miraculous pool, a church was built in his honour and to this day one of my neighbours, preferring the saint's water to that of the Welsh Water Authority, fills her flagons with it.

So my walk begins in spiritual circumstances. Past the church I go, and across the churchyard rich in poetical Welsh epitaphs, and there before me are the crumbled grey walls of St Cybi's cell. I stop for a moment, as a rule, to stare into his dark quiet pool, and to wonder at all the centuries of faith, credulity and gratitude that make it still feel sacred; but pagan that I am myself, for me the most inspiriting stage of my venture comes next. Immediately after the holy well the track ascends into a steep hanging wood of beeches and oaks, floored with turf and occasional boulders, and shadowy even on the sunniest day. Here I imagine the saint retreated for solitude, when the pious press grew too much for him, and there is a big rock against which I too like to prop myself, sinking into the green dapple of the place as one steps into a nicely steaming bubble bath.

The wood is always free of people, but it is never empty. I feel its private life flourishing all around me. Beetles scurry, squirrels scamper, worms squirm, flies buzz. I expect a fox or two lives somewhere there, perhaps there are badgers, certainly buzzards circle watchfully above the trees and sometimes I hear the expostulation of a raven. I feel absolutely at ease in that wood. It is all real, and all good.

Across a bare patch of grassland next, frequented by morose-looking sheep, and then I come to the part of the excursion I least enjoy – the *memento mori* that all the best mountain expeditions offer somewhere along the way. Ages before Cybi found this place some people older than history built themselves a fort around its crest. Who they were, only presumptuous scholars claim to know, but their grey defensive walls, tumbled this way and that now in a chaos of stones, are still grimly formidable.

I hate these remains, chiefly because they speak only of extinction. Some prehistoric sites seem to me quite homely, and are instantly evocative of busy times and fortunes long ago. Not the fortress walls of Pentyrch. They are more than just negatively lifeless. They are positively dead. They seem to suggest that the end of all things is to be just like them, bleached grey and loveless on a hilltop somewhere. I leap over them as fast as I can, praying that I am not going to break my leg in some crevice among them, and be left there to die of starvation, or be eaten by sheep.

But I'm not dead yet. It is only a few minutes more to the top of
the hill, and there I am restored by a very opposite sensation. I am
careful never to look over my shoulder as I make the ascent of
Bryn Pentyrch, so that when I reach the summit the grand prospect
that awaits me comes as a never-failing surprise. If that immemorial
fort was death petrified, all around me now is life itself. Eastward
to the mountains, westward to the island of Enlli, south and north
to the seas beyond our narrow peninsula, Wales lies there to my
besotted eyes resplendent whatever the weather. There are yachts
perhaps in Pwllheli Bay, and cars scurrying along the coast road
far below, and smoke rises from the chimneys of solitary farms,
and dogs bark in the distance, and a fine high wind sweeps out of
the Eryri mountains to tingle my cheeks and blow my hair about.
Away to the south-east, if the day is clear enough, I can see the
silent summit of Arenig Fawr – and beyond it, I swear, shimmering
in a rosy sun, its brother Canigou.

So I go down again like an adventurer back from some far
greater achievement: down through the lugubrious masonry of the
ancients, down through the fructifying forest, past the holy well,
through the churchyard and home, newly inspired, to have another
go at that particularly recalcitrant paragraph towards the end of
Chapter Four.

28
Doing what Waring Did

Having a taste for the hole-in-corner, every few years I visit Trieste on the Adriatic. Its surreptitious air rejuvenates me. It rejuvenated Browning's Waring, too, you may remember, for having disappeared from the tedium of London literary society he turned up wearing a wide straw hat and a black kerchief in the stern of a Trieste bum-boat – glimpsed just for a fleeting moment, from the deck of an inbound brig, before his little craft sped off 'as with a bound, into the rosy and golden half o'the sky'. I suppose we all get tired sometimes of living in the open, where everything is plain to see and we ourselves are obvious, and when I feel this sporadic impulse to enter an existence more opaque, I do what Waring did.

Trieste, which is Triest in the German orthography, Trst in the Slav, lies introspectively in one of Europe's obscurer corners. It was the first city in the whole world that I ever got to know, and the first that ever made me feel I had somehow become a part of it. Physically it is not at all a nook-and-cranny sort of place. On the contrary, it is rather spectacular, set on a wide bay with a castle on one promontory, a lighthouse on another, and a handsome tree-lined promenade running away in a wide curve along its waterfront. Its climate, too, is nothing if not explicit – furiously hot in high summer, swept by mighty winds in winter – and its manner is on the whole gentlemanly and generous. But it is also enticingly ambiguous of flavour, like some very sophisticated drink, stopping short of sour but very far from sweet. That is why I go there.

Trieste's history has been rankled by disappointment. Standing at the crook of the Adriatic, where nowadays Italy meets Yugoslavia, once it was the chief port of the entire Austro-Hungarian dominion, and Vienna's gateway to the sea. It was left forlorn by the collapse of the Habsburg Empire after the First World War, and has staggered on since then as an Italian seaport in a more or less permanent condition of uncertainty.

The very buildings of its city centre convey a sense of regret, and entice me into moods of poetic melancholy. Once the headquarters of immense corporations and powerful bureaucracies, still big, ornate and pompously crested, they stand there like so many mummified grandees, their consequence long since sucked out of them, only their reputations embalmed. They look rich on the outside, shabby within, and the life that streams around them offers something of the same effect, appearing at first sight energetic, prosperous and homogeneous, but turning out to be, on longer acquaintance, anything but.

I love to wander purposeless through the streets of Trieste, whistling: I have always been a whistler, and these deceptive boulevards, at once louche and grandiose, seem particularly to suit what is now a dying practice – when did you last hear a whistler in the street? Downtown Trieste is as noisy as any other Italian city, and the wide central quay beside the harbour is thronged with the parked cars of half europe, but the traffic has its own particular and perverse excitement. It is all on its way to somewhere else: to Venice in the west, to Yugoslavia, Hungary, Bulgaria in the east, northwards to Austria, Germany and Switzerland. Not many people visit Trieste for its own sake. not many ships dock in its port, and this air of way-station or caravan-serai, which might make another place seem particularly free and frank, only accentuates for me Trieste's compelling condition of envelopment, and makes me whistle all the more.

Although it is in Italy, the city is surrounded on three sides by the high limestone *karst* of Yugoslavia. More than that, it is inhabited by a peculiar mixture of peoples and memories, Germanic, Latin, Slav, all of whose styles and languages seem to be forever caught in its ambience, like stale air in a closet. It is all I think of as an enclave, idiosyncratic, wry, sceptical, resigned – a place where Jews were happy, until the Nazis murdered them, and where creative exiles of many kinds have found congenial refuge. As for me, it makes me feel like a Stateless wanderer, which is what I intermittently pine to be.

Also, while I don't know if it is really true, I always like to imagine that despite indigent appearances hidden currents of profit and opportunism flow through Trieste, dubious mercantile channels out of Sofia or Budapest, black-market deals with dissident Croatians. There is a roguery in the air which balances the sense of frustration, and regularly persuades me that in this equivocal backwater I might myself go further than mere indolence, and adopt a life of crime.

The geography of the city encourages me in this aspiration – occupying as it does an ideological junction, Trieste seems just made for mayhem. Its neighbouring countryside has a flinty, harsh, demanding quality that I relish, and offers me perfect locales for skullduggeries of the fancy. In particular I like to frequent the noisy inns of Bassovizza, the last village before the Yugoslav frontier to the east, which is a very Slav community, but a favourite resort of Triestinos Latin and Germanic too. These are trellised, trestle-tabled, jam-packed, often hilarious hostelries, with waiters dashing madly in all directions, and jolly groups of friends drinking beer and eating spiced quail, venison and wild boar. Up there, I like to think, I might engage in all sorts of enjoyable villainy, consorting with double agents, sharing ideas with fellow-anarchists, arranging deals in illicit jeans or splitting the profits of smuggled gold.

But no, back from Bassovizza in the evening, down the winding road from Opicina on the top of the ridge, there lie the lights of Trieste below looking altogether innocuous. I go to this city, I know, in a mood preposterously subjective. Waring disappeared there to be rid of a tired identity, and my own images of it are doubtless wishful images, heightened by time and imagination, of myself when young.

29
On Books

My mother, who preferred to read seven or eight books simultaneously, in two or three languages, left them all over the place open at her current page, propped above washbasins, recumbent on sofas, or unexpectedly on the piano music-stand. Perhaps it was the profligate intimacy of this habit, making the printed word an inescapable participant in every action of daily life, that has made the book, whether I am reading it, writing it, feeling it, smelling it, all too frequently buying it or simply possessing it, one of my own more ubiquitous delights.

My house is a house of books. As the heart of a ship is the engine-room, and the only purpose of a tank the gun, so the library which occupies its whole ground floor, gradually climbing upstairs too, is what the building is all about. It is, as the computer people say, a dedicated building.

It is not however one of those legendary book-houses that one reads about, stuffed with books in extricable confusion, like that of Canon Claude Jenkins of Christ Church during my time at Oxford, whose books were alleged to spill out into the quadrangle whenever he opened the front door. I pride myself upon the order of my library. I like to think I know where every volume is to be found, give or take a letter of the alphabet or the difference between a tall book and a short one. My neighbour the philosopher Rupert Crawshay-Williams used to urge me to stack my books, as he did, not laterally along the shelves, but vertically from the narrow shelves at the top to the deep shelves at the bottom, so that books of all sizes could be vertically adjacent. But this logical system somehow seems un-bookish to me, so that there are times when looking for a big book about Bhutan, say, I have to run my eye through Afghanistan, Nepal and even Tibet before I reach a shelf-space tall enough to hold it.

Book-lovers will understand me, and they will know too that part of the pleasure of a library lies in its very existence. 'Books do furnish a room', as the title of one of Anthony Powell's novels has it; and no decor is more satisfying than the composition of well-filled library shelves, so rich in colour and varying shapes. Until I was an undergraduate I used to leave the dust-jackets on all my new books. Then one day I observed my tutor J. I. M. Stewart (alias Michael Innes) unpacking a new book and instantly, as he threw away the packing paper, throwing away the dust-jacket too. The urbanity of this action so appealed to me that for years I did the same – libraries of jacketed books, I came to feel, looked just like bookshops, besides suggesting that you might intend to sell them yourself one day. I made an exception of books with especially beautiful jackets, and now that my library is large enough to absorb all kinds, more and more I leave the jackets on, adding not only colour and texture to the shelves, but also contributing, in a laminated, shiny sort of way, to the smell.

For the smell is an intoxication to me, especially on hot summer days when everything is dry and flinty. I am a book-sniffer. I have a Chinese wicker goat whose enamelled inside, reached by the removal of a little wicker lid, also offers me a powerfully stimulative and possibly addictive odour, but it is nothing like so habit-forming as the smell of books. I like all the literary smells, from leather to glue to old dust to new paper, and most of all I like the smell of old-fashioned American printing ink. They no longer use this fragrant substance – perhaps they don't use ink at all? – but fortunately it is very resilient, and there are a number of books in my collection which, having been printed in the United States half a century or more ago, contribute far more than their share to the aroma. H. L. Mencken's *The American Language* is one, and John Gunther's *Inside USA* another. Sometimes I take them down from their shelves just for a sniff; and as each year I sense their powers fading, so I feel my own life passing with them.

Not that this is a melancholy feeling. One can hardly be melancholy in a library of one's own. The sensation that *The American Language* and I are growing old together strikes me as touchingly enjoyable, while the brand-new cock-sure volumes which appear each week bar-coded on my shelves are like earnests of youth renewed.

As a writer of books I work to a disciplined quota, finding that the mind, like the body, welcomes regular exercise and discharge. I normally write twelve pages of typescript a day, and if it happens that the end of my twelfth page falls in the middle of a sentence, there and then I switch off the word processor, leaving the thought hanging in the air until next morning – when its uncompleted condition makes it all the easier to start work again.

However logic has not played a great part in the conception of my books. Ideas for them have generally come to me out of the blue, and I find that the first drafts of my typescripts, composed almost without thought, stream-of-consciousness style, often survive nearly without change through two subsequent and earnestly reasoned revisions. I wrote my first novel in a state of heedless euphoria, fuelled by frequent rum punches upon a beach in Barbados, and when I look back even at the most pretentious of my works, I seem to have produced them in a kind of haze. This may account for their cavalier handling of dates and their apparent inability to distinguish the points of the compass – though when I once remarked to an admiral of the Royal Navy that I could never remember whether longitude was up and over or round and about, he said he had suffered from the same difficulty throughout his career, besides not knowing how to spell or pronounce the word.

Then out of the blue too seems to come publication day, often so long after the delivery of the typescript that I am already forgetting the matter of the book, being half way through the next one. Readers can seldom imagine, but all writers know too well, how swiftly expertise can be overtaken – how deliberately indeed one tends to shrug it off the instant a book is finished, and one moves to another subject. So the moment when the advance copy arrives, years after I have conceived the book, remains one of my life's recurring excitements.

The first copy of my first book reached me when we were entertaining a friend to lunch on board our houseboat in Cairo. As I unwrapped it, to reveal its handsome dust-jacket glinting in the sun, she said to me: 'However many books you write, you'll never get quite the same thrill as you're getting now.' She was, however, wrong. I get at least as much of a thrill every time a new book arrives, and sometimes much more. The experience is generally likened to the birth of a baby, but I prefer to think of it in architectural terms: each new book seems to me like the addition of another wing or floor to the large and peculiarly asymmetrical building which is my work as a whole. How best to finish the structure often exercises my mind. I used to think I would like to cap it with something monumental, like a skyscraper tower, but my mind moves nowadays towards something less imposing – a literary folly perhaps, simply to make people smile as they pass by.

Writing books is a wonderful pleasure, but I cannot say the process is all carefree delight. I truly have no idea, when I have finished a book, whether it is good or bad; sometimes the ones I most like prove to be the weakest, and the other way round, leaving me with oddly ambivalent feelings about them all. Besides, there are always the reviews. Some writers I believe care not a fig about reviews, but I am not one of them. Reviews have a seriously unsettling effect upon me. If they are flattering they give me a swollen head, if they are derogatory they depress me terribly. John Cheever used to scrumple them up unread as soon as they arrived, but was sometimes to be seen later unscrumpling them from the waste-paper basket, and I have sometimes caught myself in the very same act – just as very occasionally, I admit it with a blush, I have written in my head extremely favourable reviews of my own books.

In any case, although in my experience phrases from reviews, whether good or bad, remain in the memory for the rest of a writer's life, the public effect of them soon fades. Unless a book has actually been strangled at birth by the critics, or does indeed deserve to be strangled, presently it outgrows the opinions of the reviewers to live happily ever after. One of my books has already survived some of its unfriendliest critics, giving me a private income still when they are mouldering in the grave; and on its thirtieth birthday, which comes up very soon, I propose to send a celebratory copy to the most contemptuous of those still living, who could think of nothing nice to say about it when it made its nervous entry into the world. Hell hath no harpy like a writer misreviewed.

But if I am methodical in the possession of books, and mechanical in the writing of them, when it comes to reading I somehow lack self-control. It is at night, in bed before sleep, that I do most of my reading for pleasure. Now at last, I say to myself, at the end of the long and often jumpy day, for the measured satisfaction of literary recreation, better prose than mine to relish, finer ideas to admire. Sometimes I promise myself I will keep a reading list, to marshal my responses for the future, and give balance to my input. I resolve to fill in gaps in my education, introducing myself to new authors, catching up on old. I resolve to have *system*.

But it never happens. When it comes to the point I find myself reading, as always, haphazardly and indiscriminately, from thriller as from poetry, from the dead and the living, classics and car magazines, in Welsh as in English, attentively or half-wandering; and my evening literature, far from bringing more ordered standards to my mind, leaves me as I turn the light out only the more gratefully bemused – rather as though, in fact, I have been reading several books at the same time. People often say I take after my mother.

30
Imperial Consolations

When I was twenty-one years old, at the end of the Second World War, I had occasion to call upon the official in charge of the township of Gaza, where Samson had destroyed the temple of Dagon above his own head, where Alexander the Great had sold everyone into slavery, and where in later years Israelis were to battle against the unreconcilable hostility of Arabs. I went through a wicker gate, I seem to remember, to reach his office, and up some steps to a verandah, and into a fan-cooled room, clean but untidy with books and papers, and there he stood waiting to receive me: a youngish Englishman in khaki drill, rather diffident, with kind blue eyes I thought and a beefy physique. It was my duty to take him in my jeep to a map-reference in the neighbouring desert where my regiment proposed to establish a tank firing range, and as he left his office he grabbed a well-worn trilby hat from a hook beside the door and put it negligently, tilted to one side, upon his head.

There was something about that hat that I greatly admired. After so long seeing Englishmen only in uniform, it seemed to me magnificently civilian, even Bohemian. Better still, it looked unassuming. Though its owner was satrap of Gaza, it seemed to imply that he suffered from no self-importance, did not impose his authority by side or rank, but relied upon his own character and the values he was entrusted to represent. I suppose on ceremonial occasions he wore the ridiculous plumed helmet of the Colonial Service, but the brown hat suited him far better; and I like to think it was the hat that first endeared me to the British Empire – not to the principal of the thing, for particularly as a Welsh patriot I cannot approve of any one nation forcibly ruling another – but to its style. The district commissioner of Gaza was the first official of the British Empire I had ever met, and he implanted in me a taste for the imperial aesthetic that has never left me.

Not long afterwards the emotions inspired by his trilby were compounded by another piece of headgear: Andrew Holden's tarboosh. Holden was an imperial official of an older generation, who had been in the Egyptian Ministry of Finance since the days of direct British control there. He had spent his whole life in the Empire's service, and represented its style no less persuasively, I thought, than the administrator of Gaza. He was married to Field Marshal Montgomery's sister, but nobody could be less showy. His only brag, one that he loved to repeat, was that it was he, carrying a bag of gold in his own hands, who had gone to the Khedive of Egypt to buy the plot of land upon which the British Embassy in Cairo now stands. Otherwise, to hear him talk, you might have assumed his career to have been one of utterly uneventful diligence, proceeding calm and even-handed through all the Byzantine machinations of Egyptian affairs; and perhaps it was.

By the time I met him Holden was an elderly and highly respected functionary, very well known in Egypt, yet he still went to work each morning by tram, clinging to the outside like any other Cairene if he could not get a seat. The amiable Egyptians, helping him up the step, would make sure he had a place on the rear platform, where he could hang on to the pole; and there I can see him now as the tram swayed and clanked its way into town, so scholarly-looking in his spectacles, so slight, so incongrously at ease – and on his head, tilted like the district commissioner's at a jaunty but not ostentatious angle, the red tarboosh which was the only badge of his commitment.

Later I played my own peripheral part in Empire. It was the time of the great withdrawal, when the British quite deliberately abandoned their vast overseas estate, starting with the key to it all, India. Seduced as I had been by those hats, and all they seemed to represent, I was of the opinion at first that the longer the imperialists hung on to their positions, the better it would be for the world. I thought that whoever replaced Andrew Holden and the man in Gaza would almost certainly be inferior. I changed my view, however, when I came to see that the imperial principle itself could no longer be upheld, and that hanging on to it for its own sake was not only unfair to the indigenes, but morally corrupting to the British.

By the 1950s the Middle East, the last great field of British imperialism, was the cockpit of the retreat, and as a newspaper correspondent there I witnessed many a miserable action and aftermath of the withdrawal: in Palestine, in Egypt, in the puppet-States of Jordan and Iraq, in Cyprus, in Aden – all former stations of Empire from which the British themselves, or their surrogates, withdrew with bitter reluctance, and often with bloodshed too. I did not at all enjoy this process. I hated to see patriots bullied and hounded, and equally I hated to see the British Army, whose task it was to fight a rearguard action, degraded by the task.

As the decline of Empires go, nevertheless, it was a humane and liberal decline. The settlers on the spot were sometimes despicable, the soldiers sometimes behaved cruelly, higher authority sometimes lied or prevaricated, but there was no such prolonged and senseless campaign of reaction as the French undertook in Indochina and Algeria. And towards the end of the 1950s I took part in a little adventure which once again fired my affection for the imperial manner of things.

This was an expedition mounted by the Sultan of Muscat, one of the British Empire's last puppets, to establish his sovereignty over the interior of the country, which he had never in his life visited, and where his authority was challenged by a rival potentate, the Imam of Oman. I say it was mounted by the Sultan, but it was instigated by the British, who wanted to make sure that he and they controlled the oil resources they hoped to lie within Oman's frontiers. The British provided officers and equipment for the Sultan's army, and diplomatic screens when necessary for all his policies. That he was an absolute despot of the old school did not perturb them. If he preferred to have slaves, to forbid tobacco and alcohol, to keep his people in a condition of medieval ignorance and poverty, to forbid the entry of all foreign ideas and deliberately maintain his country's status as one of the most inaccessible on earth, that was his business.

There is no pretending then that it was a very noble neo-imperial expedition that we undertook – the Sultan, his courtiers, his slaves, his goats, his handful of askaris and me. It was, however, the greatest fun. As it happened it was the first attempt to cross the south-eastern horn of Arabia with motor vehicles, from Dhufar on the Arabian Sea to Muscat on the Persian Gulf, and I was there as the Sultan's guest. 'Your interest to write an account of my journey is very much appreciated,' he had assured me on his crested notepaper, and I was fond of him for all his despotism. Attended by huge Sudanese, fed on goats, prayed for by holy men, threatened by contumacious tribesmen of the interior, we bounced our way across the edge of the Empty Quarter with a fine panache, often getting stuck in the sand, stopping for worship several times a day, passing through country never before seen by a European, while the little turbanned Sultan sat in the front of his truck like a bearded idol, now and then consulting the compass which he kept in a blue plastic shopping bag upon his knee.

I thought it wonderfully in the old imperial tradition, the tradition of Curzon and Gertrude Bell and the explorers of the Asian frontiers, and later I wrote a small book about the experience. A reviewer of this slight work, recognizing in it my feelings towards the style of the by then all-but-vanished imperium, said that instead of fiddling around the edges of the imperial saga, I ought to write a big assessment of the whole enterprise. Some years later I took his advice, and the work became the intellectual and artistic centre-piece of my life.

It was specifically the Victorian Empire that I set out to evoke in my trilogy *Pax Britannica*, from its beginnings in the 1830s to what I took to be its true symbolic ending, the death of Churchill in 1965. Fortunately there were still many survivors about, some of them old enough to remember the very climax of the whole adventure, the years around the turn of the century when British power was ubiquitous, and British imperialists were at work on frontiers from Burma to the Yukon. Two of these ancient activists, in particular, made me feel that I was in direct contact with the spirit of Empire at its most beguiling.

The first was Hugh Boustead, whose life was like an imperial mosaic. He was the only Royal Navy officer ever publicly pardoned for desertion; he jumped ship as a midshipman in the First World War in order to see more active service on the Western Front, where he greatly distinguished himself. He was also an Olympic Pentathlon champion (1920), an Everest climber (1933), Development Secretary to the Sultan of Oman, Political Agent in Abu Dhabi and commander of the Sudan Camel Corps. I first met him as Adviser to the Sultan of Mukalla in southern Arabia, then a British Protectorate, which made him in effect the governor of the place. His house there was habitually full of Arab sheikhs, who seemed to regard it as more or less their own, sitting around all over the place, telling their beads and bombarding Boustead, whenever he happened to pass through the room, with complaints, jokes and demands; when he needed something, amid the general hubbub, he blew a blast on a silver whistle, bringing a cheerful servant in no great haste with water for a thirsty sage or more haddock for the breakfast table. Every afternoon Boustead went for a walk along the beach beside the Arabian Sea, and this was a sight to see. He would get his driver to set him down three or four miles from the city, and then walked back very fast, hands behind his back, while the Land Rover followed at a respectful distance: a stocky determined figure, tough and brown, rhythmically walking those golden sands and exchanging merry greetings with everyone along the way – crab-diggers with sacks and shovels, gaggles of small boys (who sometimes followed along behind, making funny faces), fishermen with fish on poles, the emaciated Bedouin with their strings of camels, crows pecking at their hairy humps, who now and then loped along the shore.

Boustead retired in the end to Tangier, taking with him an Arab servant, complete with family, whom he sent to Germany for a course in the maintenance of his Volkswagen camper, to England for a course in cookery (and to whom he eventually left his house). He was the kindest and most entertaining of imperialists – the kind of whom the American philosopher George Santayana once said: 'Never since the heroic days of Greece has the world had such a sweet, just, boyish master.' I associate him always with a few characteristic phrases that he loved to use. One was 'It's all your fault', uttered with such wry affection that when he retired from the Sudan Camel Corps his fellow officers had it inscribed on the bottom of his presentation silver salver. Another was the quotation he wrote for me in the fly-leaf of his autobiography:

How do I know that my youth is spent?
My get-up-and-go has got-up-and-went.

And the third was the death-bed advice he claimed to have been given by his expiring father. Raising himself with difficulty from his pillow, it seems, the patriarch managed to gasp one last sentence of counsel to his son: '*Never live in the Thames Valley.*'

My second old stalwart was F. M. Bailey, whom I met in his last years at his home in Norfolk. He was the imperial adventurer incarnate. Nobody had adventures like F. M. Bailey! He had solved the problem of the Tsangpo Gorges. He had discovered a new kind of poppy and identified a hitherto unsuspected shrew. He had been a spy in Tibet, a double agent in Russian Turkestan, a diplomat in Nepal and a confidential friend of the Dalai Lama. By the time I met him, after so many years in the back of beyond he had been turned by some weird alchemy into a kind of Tartar or Mongolian, his cheek-bones curiously heightened, his eyes aslant and his skin peculiarly like parchment.

This wonderful life he had led entirely under the auspices of the Empire, which he had served as army officer (he had fought at Ypres and at Gallipoli), as intelligence agent and as political representative. I greatly envied him. How marvellous to have had such excitement in a cause, and a cause which you considered (as Bailey unquestionably did consider it) fair, honourable and useful! This was functional adventuring, I thought, not mere dilettantism – adventure as a profession, and with a purpose. When F. M. Bailey, caught by a sudden snowslide in Tibet, saved himself from annihilation by the skilful manipulation of his butterfly net, he was just doing his job. When his father once sent him a cable saying simply WARN BAILEY MASSACRE SADIYA, Bailey merely commented that it 'failed to say who had massacred whom, or why', and left it at that.

During the ten years during which I wrote my Empire work I came to feel like this about the imperial style as a whole, and to see in all its manifestations, its architecture, its literature, its art, its fashion and even at a pinch its ceremonial, an aesthetic enviably functional and frank. I had grown up during a period when everything Victorian was generally derided, but I came to see how powerfully up-to-date it had all seemed even to my own parents, when they were children. To them the style of Empire had been a popular craze, like the Nazi craze among young Germans later, or perhaps the craze of Beatleism to my own children's generation. Everybody had tapped its feet to its martial melodies, responded with a chill of the spine to its stirring poems, and waved its flags when processions went by. So far as I know none of my forebears had anything to do with the imperial mission, and indeed they generally disliked anything that smacked of jingo, even down to Boy Scouts; yet I do not doubt that they felt a tremor of pride when Dame Clara Butt sang 'Land of Hope and Glory' at the Albert Hall.

Sceptically but none the less enjoyably, I have learnt to share some of those emotions in hindsight. I love to find Empire showing in the buildings of England – to find deep in the lush and trendy Cotswolds, for instance, the eastern pleasure-palace of Sezincote, golden dome and tropic eave, shrine and oriental bridge among the green meadows. Better still, elsewhere in the world I am still excited by the memorials of the Empire-builders, and in this kind my favourite is the Victoria Railway Terminal at Bombay, a very prodigy of imperial good intentions, whose tower is vaguely Oxonian, whose windows are cathedral-like, and whose snake and monkey gargoyles are balanced by medallions of worthies like Queen Victoria and the Chairman of the Great Peninsular Railway. I was riding in a bus once past this wonderful structure when an Englishman, sitting on the seat behind, pointed out to me a portrait of his own grandfather, sculpted above the main gate – the Marquess of Dufferin and Ava, Viceroy of the day.

I would hate to live among it myself, but I have also learnt to cherish from a distance the imperial decor which I can myself dimly remember from other peoples' houses of my childhood. Elephant tusks seem to have been essential to this decorative trend, elephant feet too if possible, and there must be Benares brass about, and heavy hanging brocades, and a thick superstructure of rugs, swords and eastern armour. Strange stuffed birds should stare from glass cases, African idols brood in alcoves, and the impact was heightened if more personal trophies could be inserted among the *objets trouvés*: the actual ink-well, possibly, from which Uncle Henry had signed his treaty with the Nawab, or, as I remember seeing suspended above a doorway in a house in Powys, a stick like a boomerang that had belonged to the Mad Mullah of Somaliland.

I have no primitive weapons or bits of elephant at home, but I do have on my wall a signed print by Elizabeth Butler, entitled *The Survivor*, which commemorates a tragic moment of British imperial history: the return to Jellalabad in 1842 of Surgeon-Captain Brydon, solitary survivor of the annihilated army of the Indus. The imperialists loved such art. Every adventure found its painter, and even punitive missions or geological expeditions were immortalized in careful draughtsmanship. Nobody though was quite like Elizabeth Butler, whose vast and often lethal compositions imprinted themselves upon the vision of the nation, and would stand for ever, on many a wall besides my own, as archetypal artefacts of the imperial moment.

Lady Butler got all the buttons, ribbons and guns right, and she did not flinch from the realities of the imperial mission. My own example of her work represents only one exhausted officer on his even more exhausted pony, but most of her pictures are full of maimed, bandaged or actually dead Britons sprawled upon barricades or undergoing frightful bombardments. There was a kind of picture popular then which concerned itself with the frailties of mankind, and offered didactic allegories of human failure. It was not Elizabeth Butler's kind. In her pictures the stiff upper lip never weakens. Even after the most appalling consequences of military error the soldiers can always summon a faint but manly cheer, and when I look up at *The Survivor* from my writing-table I can just see in its background the British garrison of Jellalabad, like the army of Heaven, sallying forth to succour the doctor and his pony.

Of course I have been seduced by the glamour of it all. I am moved to see those fortresses of Empire upon the distant frontiers, and to imagine the sahibs, swathed about in blinding cummerbunds, coated in sky-blue, turbanned and high-booted as they went about their imperial business.

God knows I am not impervious to the waste and sadness of it all. Few moments in my life have chilled me more than the moment when an assistant at the British Museum Library placed in my hands the original manuscript of General Gordon's diaries, their

163

last pages written at Khartoum in the very hours before his death. I could almost feel the heat of his roof-top then, smell the dust and the death and the gunpowder, hear the shouting below and feel for myself how fanatic the imperial convictions could become. Besides, nobody who has wandered the imperial graveyards, with their hundreds of thousands of homesick young people dead in an unnecessary cause in a distant country, fighting an enemy there was no need to fight, or killed by a climate there was no need to endure – surely nobody who has shed a tear among the tombstones of Empire could be an imperialist still. 'One more picture like this,' said General Sir William Butler to his wife the artist, inspecting her enthusiastic representation of the siege at Rorke's Drift, 'and you will drive me mad.'

I am glad it is all over, for it was really all a huge illusion, behind which truth took shelter. The images of Empire have soon faded, and only a few artists and aficionados, like me, have found themselves fired by the old aesthetic, or have revived it in nostalgic pastiche. The tragedies of greater wars, the humiliations of decline, the rise of new values, dimmed the dazzle of the old adventure. Commissioners of quite other kinds assumed authority in Gaza, and it is many a long year since an Englishman in a tarboosh went to work on a Cairo tram. So be it. The Empire's time was past. All the same, something went out of the British vision then: greys, greens and half-tones drove the gold away.

31
The Walk of Walks

The human race was designed, in my opinion, not to jog for its physical recreation, but to walk. Most people look silly jogging, but one can walk with swank, one can walk with style, one can feel like General de Gaulle parading down the Champs-Elysées, one can observe with dignity the passing scene, one can converse without panting, smile without strain, and take one's exercise with the composure evolution evidently intended, when it stood us on two legs and made us lords of nature.

Once on a French national holiday, I really did walk down the middle of the Champs-Elysées, feeling terrifically Gaullist, and I have felt distinctly exalted too walking over Brooklyn Bridge on a fine windy morning, and walking briskly around the lakes at Blenheim, and for that matter walking the high ridges above my *dacha* in the Black Mountains of Wales. But of all the promenades I know, one more than any other seems to me the walk of walks. It is the path that runs around Victoria Peak – 'the Peak' for short – on the island of Hong Kong. When I am in that demanding colony I do the Peak walk every morning before breakfast, and I come down to my corn flakes in the city feeling not just the fitter for it, but the more serene too – as if, striding rhythmically as I do around the half-hour circuit of the hill, I have started the day with a commitment to the organic order of things.

The Peak itself is not generally considered a metaphor for natural propriety. It was developed, towards the end of the nineteenth century, as a hill station for the British colonists of Hong Kong, and for many years preserved a rigid racial segregation – only in the 1930s was the first Chinese allowed to build a house there, and he was not only half-European anyway, but enormously rich as well. The higher you lived, the grander you were, and the more absolutely you looked down, figuratively as physically, upon lesser residents below.

But snobby and racialist though the British Empire could be, it had a fine eye for landscape, and was particularly expert at pleasaunces. The path its engineers built around the Peak, through its bowers of jasmine and wild indigo, daphne, rhododendron and shiny wax trees, is a classic example of the *genre*. Part of it is called Harlech Road, part of it Lugard Road, but it is really hardly more than a lane, and though here and there along it villas lie half-hidden in shrubberies, and cars are parked discreetly in lay-bys, for the most part it remains a secluded country walk of the subtropical imperial variety.

Sometimes I find the path all but obliterated by Hong Kong's notorious morning mists. Everything drips with damp then, and there seems to be nobody alive up there but me. More generally all is fresh and dewy in the early morning. Butterflies waver about my path, kites and long-tailed magpies swoop, and among the trees the racket of the cicadas falls torrent-like about me. As I progress terrific vistas reveal themselves. Now I see the island-studded reaches of the south, away down the blue-grey China coast. Half a mile later, and there lie the vast fleets of merchantmen at their anchors in the outer anchorage, and a jetfoil is streaming away towards the Pearl River estuary, and the hills of Kowloon stand in misty silhouette across the water. Finally through a gap in the trees I see the city itself precipitously far below, stirring tremendously in the morning. The early sun is catching its windows, the ferries are coming and going already, the traffic hurries to work across fly-over and highway. Seen from this high eyrie, in the cool of the early day, it seems to me like a city in someone else's imagination – like the city Satan showed Jesus, from the top of another mountain.

Even better than the prospects are the people, for soon after daybreak the Peak path is usually full of other exercisers, pilgrims of the morning easing themselves into the day. They are very varied. There are courteous Chinese gentlemen wearing Walkman headsets and carrying walking sticks, who smile and slightly bow. There are svelte European ladies exercising svelter dogs. There are groups of Chinese students, three or four abreast, chattering and laughing and waving to me as they pass. There are gentlemanly Britons who look like judges, and tall Americans who look like graduates of Harvard Business School.

Most numerous, most dedicated, more suitable of all, there are scores of Chinese men and women, mostly elderly, engaged in the slow and enigmatic system of exercise called Tai Ji Quan, the Great Ultimate Fist. All along the path I see them as I pace by, sometimes alone and silent, sometimes shouting messages to one another across the stillness of a gully, and the stylized grace of their exertions, the measured shadow-boxing, the expression of inner deliberation as they stretch their limbs or twist their hands, haunts me always with the power of the Chinese mystery.

For a mystery it remains, and though it is an imperial track I have been following, built by expatriate Britons to satisfy their own alien urges, still one of the glories of the Peak walk is its illumination by the presence of China – which on these occasions often really does seem to me, as the ancient Chinese so obdurately declared it, the focus and paradigm of the world. Chinese are those birds and flowers around me, Chinese those contoured islands, the hills of China bound the northern horizon and the energy which now, as the sun rides about the ridge and I reach the end of the circuit comes to me as a distant rumble from the city beneath – that tireless energy is above all a Chinese mechanism.

An influential Chinese device, as influential in Hong Kong as it was in the China of the Manchus, is the philosophical system called *feng shui*, literally 'wind and water' – the ancient art of balance and placement. It decrees how all man's constructions, his buildings in life, his graves in death, should be situated in the context of nature itself.

The British empire-builders, when they laid out Harlech and Lugard roads, were certainly not deliberately honouring the concept of *feng shui*, which they would doubtless have dismissed as heathen superstition, but their route around Victoria Peak seems magically to obey it anyway. The path never disturbs the character of the hillside. It never seems to jar. It follows the 400-metre contour line courteously, as though not to disturb the spirits of the place, and its vistas north, south, east and west are like views allegorically opening upon life itself. The butterflies are perfectly at home along its course. Beside it the trees seem to grow affectionately.

No wonder those devotees of the Great Ultimate Fist go to the Peak to practise their stately gyrations; and no wonder that I find my morning exercise up there more than just a physical refreshment, but a tonic for all the senses. Only a fool would *run* around such a belvedere; it is just made for that happy reconciliation of mind and body, rest and labour, the walk before breakfast.

32
Looking at Things

When I was very small a stranger asked if he might look through my telescope, in those days my most prized possession except for my cat. 'What can you see through it?' he wanted to know, and I answered him scornfully, 'Just what you see anyway,' I said, 'only bigger.'

I can feel his disappointment still, for I think he expected some quainter or more quotable response from the child all alone with a spyglass on a hill above the sea. But the truth was that I was not looking for faery realms, only identifying passing ships for my roster ('Steamship MAIDSTONE 5,500 tons, registered Bristol, Jamaica banana-and-passenger trade'). My telescope fulfilled no symbolic function for me, and as a matter of fact it was a long time before, ships apart, I learned the real pleasure of looking at things. Perhaps it was the Welsh in me – Wales has always been better at sounds than at sights – or perhaps it was the Quaker legacy. Whatever the cause, my visual powers were long in abeyance. I moved through the most beautiful scenes of my childhood, it seems to me now, observing but seldom perceiving – the sea was only a tidal fact, the hills were merely geographical features, and I looked at the world simply as a work of reference. My vision was altogether literal, and chiefly concerned with tonnage deadweight.

Having failed in early life to get much out of landscapes and seascapes, I was no more successful in appreciating furniture, the first *objets d'art* to which most of us are exposed. I never did understand the preoccupation of adults with chairs and tables, and to this day I cannot take them very seriously. A chair is a thing for sitting on, a bed is a thing for sleeping in. If they look handsome

169

well and good, if not they are disposable anyway. Like clouds, they come and go. The best houses, for my tastes, largely disregard their furniture, leaving it simply lying about to be used – or if they happen to be in Japan, have virtually no furniture anyway.

I preferred looking at cars, and still do. The motor-car is disposable too, Heaven knows, and moves in and out of fashion far more arbitrarily than any furniture, but it has to it more historical meaning than your most elaborate Louis XIV commode. The car is not simply social index. It is the state of engineering and electronics, it is the economic condition of nations, it is the psychology of whole people and periods. A 1912 Bugatti is much more interesting than a 1680 commode; more beautiful, too.

Think of the disparity of talent! There sits your furniture craftsman in his workshop, chipping away; an artist perhaps in shape and ornamentation; skilful with glues, knowledgeable about varnish, able to make an object at once useful and good to see. But take your most ordinary car – take your Toyota, take your Volkswagen – and consider the prodigious concentration of talent embodied in that one machine! The inventor and the engineer, the stylist and the tool-maker, the specialists in steel stress, and paint, and glass, and rubber, the ergonomists, the upholsterers, the robot-designers! When I look at a Chippendale sofa I see, with admiration, Mr Chippendale; but when I see a Honda in the street I see all those gifts and labours passing by – rather as, when I hear the music of some great stage show, I like to remember the battalions of contributors, lyricists to choreographers to dressers, whose work is celebrated in the final joyous chord.

It took me time to learn to look at pictures. I enjoyed an art gallery now and then, and relished the delight of seeing in the original a painting I had always known from place-mat or Christmas card. I chiefly liked pictures of places I knew, like preferring music whose tunes one knows. All this was changed for ever, however, when, long ago in Venice, I fell beneath the spell of Giorgione.

One of the gifts of soldiering in Italy was the chance to see, as in a rough-and-tumble Grand Tour, some of the greatest of paintings in their proper setting. I had already been introduced on their home ground to Leonardo, Botticelli and Titian. I had valued the experience, and still feel that in an ideal world all works of art would be returned to their countries of origin. But I felt no very profound response until I found myself standing in front of Giorgione's *La Tempesta*, 'The Tempest'. This peculiar masterpiece affected me most deeply. It was not merely its subject that fascinated me with its sense of permanently suspended enigma; I felt too, in a way I had never felt before, that I was in the actual presence of the artist. It seemed to me a haunted picture, around which Giorgione himself hovered wraith-like and tantalizing.

Since then I have seen almost every Giorgione in the world – almost every one, that is, listed with certainty in the Rizzoli catalogue, not to mention scores of pictures more dubiously attributed to him. From Leningrad to Washington, Oxford to Budapest I have pursued his enigmatic genius, and I have strong feelings about the authenticity of paintings that hang above his name. I swear I can tell if a picture is really his – if he is present, that is, as he was that revelatory day before *La Tempesta*, if I can sense his smoky concentration there, if I can glimpse his secret half-smile somewhere in the oils, or imagine his tap upon my shoulder. Few painters are less known as men than Giorgione, but I feel I am his intimate, and whenever I see one of his intenser masterpieces a delicious satisfaction seizes me. It is as though, not to put too fine a point upon it, through Giorgione I am in touch with God.

This obsession has put a very different complexion upon my art appreciation. No other painter has had quite that same effect upon me (though since Shakespeare often does, I have come to assume that he and Giorgione are one and the same person), but I have learnt to look at all great pictures not just as works of art, but as keys or shutters, giving access to altogether different sensations. My responses bear little relation to the judgement of experts, and I feel liberated from the restraints of taste. It is not that I Know What I Like, rather that I know what I feel. Sometimes I am much moved by a picture I do not like at all, and sometimes some universally accepted prodigy, whose beauty I myself marvel at, unaccountably leaves me cold. Looking at pictures can be more than seeing; just as, I now know, there is more to a passing steamship than its port of registry.

171

But grander at least in principle than a painting, certainly loftier than a car and nobler than a sofa, seems to be a building. It is more like a work of nature than of human hands. It has its cliffs and its plateaux, its steeps and its shallows, its caves and its tunnels and its belvederes. A good building, of whatever style or period, is complete to itself. It looks as though one might pick it up like a model, without fear of its bending in the middle or cracking at the corners. It is also at ease with the natural order of things. Bad architecture looks artificial, good architecture looks organic, so that your second-rate skyscraper, which seems merely to have been taken out of a packing-case and stood up somewhere, is infinitely less majestic than your old mountain farm, lying in the flank of a hill like a geological out-crop.

I first learnt to look at buildings in Cairo. I worked in the evenings then, and in the blazing afternoons, when the city lay for the most part torpid in siesta, my love and I would drive up to the medieval quarter of the capital and explore, one by one, its incomparable assembly of medieval mosques. We were originally inspired to this by the architectural historian K. A. C. Creswell, a passionate and unrivalled authority on early Islamic buildings. I greatly admired this remarkable man, who had devoted his entire life to his esoteric speciality, who lived austerely upstairs in a drab apartment building in the middle of the old quarter, and who was later alleged, during the xenophobic Cairo riots of 1951, to have awaited his probable murder lying in a hot bath reading a scholarly book with a loaded revolver beside him. That somebody could spend a lifetime studying, *in situ*, so alien and exotic a class of structure seemed to me half magical, and I determined at least to strike up an acquaintance with the structures that Creswell knew in such minute detail.

As a result to this day no buildings stir me quite so marvellously as do the mosques of medieval Islam. I began with the mosques of Cairo, side by side with dome, pinnacle and minaret along the medieval highway, Qasabat al-Qahira, which was the central thoroughfare of the Thousand And One Nights, but over the years I extended my explorations to cover most of the great buildings of Islam. If buildings alone were faith, I would have become a Muslim long ago. Whether resting in the shadowy arcades of the Great Mosque at Damascus, where no spider ever spins his web, or wandering among the chequered arches of Cordoba, or sitting beneath the trees outside the Dome of the Rock, the architecture of Islam was to inspire in me countless moments of gratitude and serenity. It seemed to me like the symbol of a great fraternal association, reaching out across the world, Marrakesh to Istanbul to Jerusalem to Delhi, to pass the traveller safely from one shelter to the next. It has never disturbed me that Muslims may think my pagan loyalty a trifle blasphemous: the buildings know better, and when at the Blue Mosque in Istanbul a scowling worshipper, spotting me entranced but clearly infidel by the door, strode across and told me idiomatically to beat it, beat it I did without remonstrance.

The mosque is half-way to the town. Far more than Christian or Jewish structures, it was intended from its tented start to be the centre of public life: place of worship, place of assembly, university, washplace, law court, social security office – from the mosque was administered my favourite of all social services, the medieval charity which repaid household servants the cost of crockery they had broken. I grew accustomed to thinking of mosques not simply as buildings, but as communities; and these being the structures that first engaged my interest, it was perhaps only natural that in time I should graduate to looking at cities. When I was the editor of one of the Oxford undergraduate magazines I wrote to various eminences asking, in the fashion of the day, if they thought an Oxford education was worth having. The best reply came from Field Marshal Lord Wavell, a beloved but not invariably victorious general banished by Churchill to be Viceroy of India. He had lately published a substantial anthology of poems all of which he knew by heart, and it was because I much admired this facility, and also because I shared (as I still do) his simple tastes in poesy, that I had invited his comment. He said the one good reason for going up to Oxford was the privilege of living among its architecture. I agree with him, and later I came to feel that of all man's works, the most glorious to look at, and paradoxically the nearest to nature itself, were the cities. If they happen to contain a few Giorgiones and a couple of Fatimid mosques, so much the better, but just the distant view of almost any one of them, strewn with lights at night-time, sprawling hazed, towered and preferably waterfronted in the day, is enough to make my sensibilities tingle.

I would guess that for most of us the ideal city, fiction apart, is represented by Florence. The towers are there, the river flows benignly, there are no mosques indeed but at least six Giorgiones, several of which I accept as authentic. I first reached this city spectacularly, free-wheeling down the long hill from Fiesole in an armoured scout car whose transmission had broken, but I thought it at its most magnificent when, thirty years later, I arrived there one fine day to find the skyline beyond the Arno punctuated by the bulbous shapes of a Henry Moore exhibition, its works brought from all over the world to this home of Michelangelo. This, I thought, is how a city should be, its look and its function, its history and its personality all inextricably blended.

Visually the modern equivalent, I think, is Chicago, the most handsome of all twentieth-century cities, and the most generally underestimated. Some of the greatest contemporary architects have embellished its city centre, and the ensemble is given denseness and surprise by the wayward passage of the Chicago River, softening the street grid, and by the curving shoreline of Lake Michigan which bounds it. I very much covet the beautifully designed and moulded pavilions from which the bridge-tenders of Chicago open and close the bridges over the river; from those glassy eyries one can see all around a matchless exhibition of modern building, skyscrapers severe and Gothically ornamented, high and hefty warehouses, a tapering flat-topped tower which looks like an altar, the vast chunky mass of the Sears Building, its summit often half-lost in cloud, which is the tallest building mankind has ever erected.

Such places offer me the best of my looking pleasures: wandering around fine streets, sitting at corner cafés watching the play of contrast between the transient and the permanent, sketching incompetent city-scapes. But I recognize that just as the appearance of pictures can be misleading, so the look of cities is not enough. Some of the very finest are lacking in personality – even contemporary Chicago is short on conviction – while there are others, shabby and undistinguished, which possess an unmistakable inner greatness. Looking at cities, learning to possess them in a more absolute or intuitive way, has taught me a lot about looking at life, and if that man came to me now wanting to see through my telescope, I would be fancier in my response.

33
A Night on an Island

Few pleasures I know are more perfectly proportioned than a single night upon the Venetian island of Torcello – the one whose stalwart campanile you see, beyond the leaning tower of Burano, farthest away of all in the northern reaches of the lagoon. It is one of life's rules that most pleasures are too much of a good thing. They go on too long (like opera), they fill you up too much (like plum pudding), they are too wide like America or too hungry like St Bernard dogs. Only the very best of them come and go lightly, leaving you satisfied but not sated, with the sweet aftertaste in the mind that follows your awakening from a happy dream.

For me just such a pleasure is the pleasure of a night in Torcello, even in these times of touristic overkill. By definition it cannot last too long and by geography it cannot be too overwhelming, for the island is only about a mile around, has a permanent population of less than a hundred, and contains at the most a couple of dozen buildings. There are no cars on it, and no paved roads. That campanile greets its visitors with an easy-going tolerance still, knowing that though they may be here today, they will almost certainly be gone before tomorrow.

What I like to do is to board the slinky excursion launch which, every summer day at noon, takes the international tourists out from Venice for lunch at the Locanda Cipriani, the island's long-celebrated hostelry. This gives me a flashy re-entry to Torcello, all among the rich and famous (for if they're not really famous, for the Cipriani lunch they'd better be fairly rich).

The experience offers a piquant mixture of sensations. The launch sails cautiously up the long narrow creek which is the main

street of Torcello, beneath a bridge without a parapet alleged to
have been designed by the Devil, until it reaches the fulcrum of
relative bustle – a moored boat or two, a few spectators hanging
around – which marks the presence of the locanda. This looks like
a modest country tavern. Outside it a few locals sit dozily over
glasses of red wine beneath the quayside pergola. Inside there is
a garden of flowers, vines and vegetables, floated among by
swallowtail butterflies and supervised by the noble cathedral tower
just over the wall.

But in the dappled shade of the restaurant everything is vigorous
greed and gobble, confident accents Parisian, Japanese or New
Yorker, gine-fizzes and scampi and shrill laughter between tables.
It is like a morality play. When I watch the great pleasure-launch
sailing away again after the meal, all sun-glasses, designer pants
and now vinous badinage, it is as though the great hard world itself
is departing the island, leaving me naïve upon its shore.

Not that Torcello is deserted in the afternoon. Not at all. The rich
and famous may have gone pulsating away, but the more modest
holiday-makers, those who have come on the public water-bus, now
stroll everywhere around the place. On the green piazza beyond the
restaurant elderly women in straw hats and floral dresses sell lace
from a parade of canopied stalls, rather as though they are offering
sacred souvenirs at a place of pilgrimage. Children burble about
the green, playing ball beneath Romanesque arcades, dangling their
legs from the rough-hewn stone seat once popularly supposed to
have been the throne of Attila the Hun. The attendant at the
public lavatories, behind the small museum, comfortably reads a
paperback on a kitchen chair in the sunshine, while young people
with backpacks sit cross-legged here and there singing gently dis-
cordant folk-songs.

They come and go in waves through the afternoon, as the boats
from Venice come and go, strolling leisurely up the long path from
the landing-stage, hilariously running down it when they see the
upper-works of the *vaporetto* sliding up the waterway beyond the
foliage. By the early evening they are gone too. The lace ladies are
tying canvas sheets over their stalls. Attila's throne is empty and
the lavatory attendant has disappeared, locking up behind her. A

hush descends upon the island and the few score souls that remain upon it. It is time to go for an evening walk.

A man told me once that he found Torcello 'dead as old bones'. He was speaking, though, as a Londoner, to whom such a half-abandoned place, once a thriving municipality with heaps of money, may well offer funereal vibrations. Actually by the standard of these generally sterile waters Torcello is like an animated oasis.

Dusty lanes take me through its fields, past brackish back-canals, through plantations of sun-flowers sagging with the weight of their blossom, beside meadows of indeterminate vegetables and indefinable salad plants, where solitary men are still labouring away with hoes in the gloaming, or tinkering with mechanical cultivators. Here and there a homestead stands in its garden rich in the blues and yellows of homely cottage flowers. Up a reedy creek a fisherman rows his boat from the lagoon, standing cross-oared in the old Venetian way.

Dead as bones indeed! Tadpoles squirm in the little rivulets, beetles stalk the grasses, seabirds squawk, hens and pigeons scrabble in yards, ginger cats eye me, dogs bark out of sight, lizards flick on fencing-posts, tall asphodels stir in the breeze from the Adriatic. A distant bell rings across the lagoon, from Burano perhaps, or from the cypress-shrouded monastery of San Francesco del Deserto, and with a laborious gasp the great bell of Torcello itself awakens to boom mellow and melancholy through the twilight.

So night falls, and I feel myself enfolded in velvet privacy among the waters. All alone I wander after dinner through the quiet shadowy monuments of Torcello's lost consequence, its domes and its arcades, its crumbled pillars and indecipherable plaques, its campanile half-hidden in the darkness above. There is nobody about but me, unless some of those back-packers have unrolled their sleeping-bags beneath the cathedral cloister; only me, the mosquitos, the frogs which leap hilarious around my feet and the little bats that forage in and out of the lamplight.

In the morning the swallows have taken over, whirling dizzily around the bell-tower and the chimney-pots. Now, after breakfast in the locanda garden, I look once more at the monuments. I have known them for nearly forty-five years, but I feel it my duty. Besides, they are not only few, but marvellous. It was to this sedgy island, fifteen centuries ago, that the first of all the Venetians came as fugitives; the little cluster of buildings that is Torcello now represents the true beginning of all that we mean, all the dazzle and the beauty, all the power and the fizz and the sadness, when we speak the name of Venice.

What a claim! And what monuments, concentrated as they are within the space of a couple of hundred yards! Cool and calm is the simple domed form of the church of Santa Fosca, as though some lovely outhouse, a dairy, a princely stable, has been converted for holy use. Infinitely touching is the lonely figure of the Madonna, high in her mosaic apse, which greets you in the bleached stoniness of the cathedral. Peculiar stone objects of unimaginable age litter the sacred purlieus, and it is a fine thing to sit on Attila's throne, before the children arrive, looking across the tiled domes to the mighty tower above. From time to time the bell whirringly assembles its energies again to announce that another Torcello hour has passed – approaching the 14 millionth hour, I hazard a calculation, since the first Venetian settled here in AD 421.

Twelve noon, it strikes. Time for a last meal at the house beside that daemonic bridge. I ate my way into Torcello with the jet set; I eat my way out with the Italians, for the people who order their sea-food salad or spaghetti with clams at the Ponte del Diavolo come mostly from Padova, Vicenza, Treviso or Venice itself. This gives the restaurant an organic, family feel, very pleasant to take with a glass of wine and one of the rough rolls which, distributed from table to table out of big wicker baskets, constitute Torcello's very bread of life. Merrily flows the conversation. Happily flows the wine. Imperceptibly turns the cycle of the island's life. I am hardly through the cheese when, looking up across the patio, I catch sight of today's boat-load of cosmopolitans, looking just like yesterday's sailing well-fed back to Venice from the locanda up the way.

Heavens, my own *vaporetto* leaves at 2.15! I pay the bill, I tip them well, I grab my bags and sprint to the landing-stage – just in time to see the humped shape of the No 12 foaming up from Burano.

And if I'm not in time? Well, I can always catch the next one; or I can start all over again, stay another night after all with the frogs, the swallows, the mosquitos and the great grunting bell of the cathedral, and see how far a rule of life can be stretched – for to tell you the truth, two nights in Torcello is a pleasure I have never tried.

34
Welsh Affections

It used to be fashionable for Welsh people to declare their love for Wales heart-on-sleeve. Their patriotism blended with the fervour of their religion, the richness of their mythology, the dark fascination of their history and the magnificence of their landscape to exude itself in manifestations of *hwyl*, that particularly Welsh kind of enthusiasm which takes its name from the sail of a ship – billowing, bulging, swelling, straining or slackening with the tempests and the calm.

Today Welshness is generally more austerely expressed, especially in English, and some academics indeed are apt to imply that there is nothing specifically Welsh to it, except an unnecessary language. The legend of it all they regard as so much blarney, the history they think of as having ended and the *hwyl* they willingly accept only if it is expressed by crowds at rugby matches. They pride themselves on their realistic, functional approach to the subject, and they shy at any whisper of romance.

I am of the older school. People and animals apart, Wales has been my supreme pleasure, and I have loved it with a showy fervour that would not have disgraced, I like to think, the most theatrically exhibitionist evangelists of the nineteenth-century Welsh chapels. I recognize that the Welsh include, as was perceived 800 years ago by their first chronicler, Giraldus Cambrensis, both the best of men and the worst of men, but this had not deterred me. I have seen it as a loving duty to celebrate Wales in all its diversity, real and imaginary, and thus to make my own contribution to the continuity of its myth.

The wind did not properly catch my sails until relatively late in life. Half Welsh, half English, emotionally or intuitively I had always preferred the Welsh side of me. The hills of South Wales, my father's country, stirred me far more than the hills of Mendip, where my mother's people came from. Preferring outsiders and oddballs anyway, I was always attracted to the idea of Wales, its separateness, its exotic language and its high spirits. However I was nurtured firmly within the English culture, with continental undertones and later American leanings. I spent much of my early life wandering the world, and I did not feel myself in the least committed to Wales. Even when I acquired a Welsh home of my own, at the end of the 1950s, I lived there in a purely Anglo-Welsh spirit. I was proud of my Welsh blood, and I wrote a good deal about the country, but I looked at it essentially with a traveller's eye, and considered its affairs generally within the context of British, European or world history, congratulating myself that I had escaped the parochialism of absolute Welshness.

It was in the 1960s that I had a letter from a man named J. E. Jones, of whom I had never heard. He lived in Cardiff and was a famous gardener, whose best-known work remains a well-loved textbook among Welsh-speaking horticulturists. He was also general secretary of the Welsh nationalist party, Plaid Cymru, the Party of Wales. Things are very different now, but in those days this organization enjoyed, among people like me, a benevolently cranky reputation. It had never succeeded in electing a member of Parliament, had little success in local elections, and intruded into our consciousness only sporadically as the sponsor of demonstrations in support of the Welsh language, a tongue of which even the most assertively Welshy of us Anglo-Welsh knew hardly a word. J. E. Jones's letter changed the course of my life.

He had read, he told me in his somewhat stilted English, pieces of mine about Wales, and knowing that I was Welsh by patrimony, was writing to suggest in me a change of attitude. I should not be writing about Wales as an outsider. I should embrace it in its fullness and make myself a true part of it. I was much moved by this unexpected call. Mr Jones, from his suburban address in Glamorgan, was hardly acting upon me like any vision on the Damascus road. I was, however, flattered that such an ultra-Welshman should consider me fit for inclusion, as it were, in his brotherhood; and more still, I was profoundly impressed by the manner of his writing – so gentle, so diffident, but still expressing I thought some great power of conviction. I took his advice, and if I have fulfilled myself anywhere, I have fulfilled myself in Welshness.

What is Welshness, you may ask with the sceptics, and who is Welsh? For myself, having severe doubts about the very existence of race, and liking to suppose myself a citizen of the world, I have come to think that anyone is Welsh who is prepared to make a sacrifice to be Welsh. I always admired the Law of the Return, in the early days of Israel, which declared that anyone who journeyed to the country and said 'I am a Jew', *was* a Jew. The same should go for Wales. Few after all would lightly abandon another identity, another nationality, to assume such equivocal citizenship as ours; if people are ready to throw off other allegiances, and devote themselves to the privilege of being Welsh, well and good, in my opinion, Welsh they shall be.

In return, they must allow themselves to be immersed in three separate Welsh influences. The first is the history of Wales, which is different from all others, which has moulded the nation's basic attitudes, and which provides much of the fascination of the Welsh condition. Politically united with England only in the sixteenth century, Wales is alive still with shades of its own past – its remote prehistoric past, expressed in standing stones and inexplicable circles, the sweet primitive churches of its Celtic past, its princely past of courts and poets, its long fight for identity against Saxon, against Norman, against English, still to be witnessed by castle and battlefield everywhere. Welsh history is intensely concentrated. Even its implications scarcely extend beyond its own coasts and borders, and its evidences are confined within the space of some 8,000 square miles of mostly mountainous country. With eyes to see you cannot miss them. Wales is like one large historical exhibition, laid out, when its monuments are not prettied up by egregious quangos, with perfect authenticity.

Secondly, initiates must subject themselves to the landscape. The terrain of Wales *is* Wales. Welsh art, Welsh architecture and in my view the Welsh consciousness itself – all are governed by the nature of the land. There are pleasant pastoral parts of Wales, and large urbanized and industrialized slabs, but the personality of the whole place is set by its hill country, which is not quite like any other. Only in parts of Spain have I ever come across country much like the mountainous mass of Wales. 'It's just like Vermont, it's just like Vermont,' an American visitor repeatedly insisted to me; but she had come on a cloudy day, and she did not realize that above the mists, above the tree line, bare tufty sheep-runs rounded by wind and age stood surveying the sea. The maze-like highlands of Wales have dictated the destiny of the country, but in their secretive and in-bred way they have dictated the character of its people too.

Finally, for aspirant Welsh citizens, there is the language. Without the language, in my view, nobody can be completely Welsh, any more than an Englishman could be considered wholly English if he knew no English. Welsh is, with Irish, the oldest living literary language in Europe, possessing a body of literature descended without a break from the sixth century – eight centuries before Chaucer. Spoken nowadays by one in five of the Welsh population, it is a language gloriously rich in idiom, and the poetry of its heyday, the princely era of the Middle Ages, includes some of the loveliest and most beguiling verses in any language – verses of a Persian charm, an English intricacy and a body of ideas and allusions that is pure Celtic.

When, at the suggestion of J. E. Jones, I unlocked the doors of my spirit to the pleasures of Welshness, I found it easy enough to respond in a newly awakened way to the land of Wales, and to its history; but the language was another matter.

Learning any language in middle age is, unless you are a natural linguist, a hard challenge. Learning Welsh seems to me the very devil. I knew only the statutory Anglo-Welsh desiderata, knew only how to pronounce the language, when I undertook my first course at a summer school at Aberystwyth. The then Secretary of State for Wales, finding that his duties must include opening the National Eisteddfod, the great annual festival of Welshness, had taken this course in the previous year, and lent me his well-thumbed and scuffed text-books in advance. He was a man of some intellectual strength, and I was not much encouraged when he told me that few experiences of his life had been more demanding than the Cwrs Carlam, the Crash Course at Aberystwyth.

I would say the same. It was not much like learning a language, more like learning how to speak. Except for borrowed words Welsh has almost nothing in common with Latin languages, and the beginner must start almost entirely from scratch. The complications of the Welsh response, affirmative or negative, the apparently random use of tenses, the complex system of mutations by which the initial letters of words change according to what went before, the unpredictable flexibility of rules – all these, coupled with an entirely unfamiliar vocabulary, mean that the student of a certain age is reduced to the level of an infant. At Aberystwyth, for the first time in thirty years, I felt myself in less than complete command of my own activities – groping to understand, often flustered and ashamed, and going to bed each night in a truly child-like state of exhaustion.

I have never mastered the language with any subtlety, and I know only one person in my circumstances who has – a diplomat whose command is so dashing that he has lately been translating poems out of the Chinese. Even so Cymraeg, the language of the Welsh, has become a constant recreation and refreshment to me. After that fearful Cwrs Carlam I took a more leisurely and much longer course at the University of Wales in Llanbedr Pont Stefan, and from time to time I restore myself with a few days at the wonderfully evocative Welsh Language Centre at Nant Gwrtheyrn in Gwynedd, an abandoned slate port at the foot of a cliff beside the sea.

I can hardly describe the curious pleasure the Welsh language has given me, and with what a sense of pride I use it, however incompetently. It has opened my eyes not only to its own vigorous beauties, but to the liberating importance of a language. I know Welsh people, fluent in both tongues, who say not an interesting thing in English, but scintillate in Welsh. I know young people, equally bilingual, whose whole personalities flower when they are talking *yr hen iaith*, the old language – as though contact with it charges their confidence like contact with some elemental force. Few things in civilization, Cymraeg has taught me to realize, are more worth preserving than a language.

185

Inevitably, long ago, all this made a Welsh nationalist of me, and I signed up as a comrade of J. E. Jones. The language in particular, but also the Welsh landscape and the sense of Welsh history – my three pillars of Welsh meaning all depend for their survival, I believe, upon Welsh political self-rule. It may be too late. The sheer numbers of English settlers swarming into Wales, most of them with no intention of modifying their English loyalties, or indeed recognizing that they have come to another country, may well spell the end of Welshness. The times are against such survivals. But it is certainly not dying yet. Welsh patriotism is robust and clever, and, who knows, the times may change.

Like many another patriot, I love to day-dream about a Wales restored entirely to itself, its own language supreme again, its own people in control. In my mind indeed for many years such a republic has existed. What a country it is! Small but self-possessed, released at last from the torments of domination, it is famous everywhere for its serene assurance, and is dedicated above all to the pursuit of personal happiness. I have given it a capital, the little sea-coast town of Machynlleth, where our President lives in very modest state, and recruited for it an army of citizen guerrillas, *sans* uniform, *sans* drill, intended only to defend the country as the Boer commandos defended theirs against the British long ago. In foreign affairs it is formally neutral, economically it is an enthusiastic member of the European Community.

The food is marvellous in my Wales of the mind, the country swarms with brilliant doctors, lawyers and journalists drawn home from England and abroad by the unique allure of the little republic. And writers, artists and musicians are not only honoured, but actually favoured by tax concessions – or would be, if there were any taxes, for just as the climate of this new Wales has been miraculously transformed into one closely approximating that of Bermuda, so by arrangements known only to myself there is in fact no need to tax anyone at all.

This is romancing, and I mean it only to make you smile. Romance of a more real kind, however, the romance that has traditionally informed the idea and the reputation of Wales, I propagate as one might promote a political philosophy. Derived as it is from my

186

three prerequisites of Welshness, I believe that it alone can give permanence to the national identity.

Of course it is essentially subjective. It is like one of those spirits which seem to exist only because a mind calls them into being. For many centuries the collective mind of Wales gave the country its legends, its dreams, its sense of immanence. Now that the national consciousness by and large thinks otherwise, I have felt it my task to help sustain into my own generation, if only in English, the tradition of the fabulists, the story-tellers, the romancers and the myth-makers, and I have written a large book about Wales to be its instrument. It is a book of romantic defiance. Perhaps later generations may resume the old infatuation, but young Welsh writers nowadays think in less sentimental terms, and I have a feeling that *The Matter of Wales* may be the last book of its kind, the last in the old tradition, the last to swell its prose and foam its cadences with the billow of *hwyl* unabashed.

The house of Wales has many mansions, all the same. 'Though it appear a little out of fashion,' said Henry V of Fluellen (alias Llewelyn), that stereotypical Welsh romantic, 'there is much care and valour in this Welshman.' How content I would be if my countrymen one day said something similar of me.

35
As to Friendship

As to friendship, life's experience has taught me that it is the fundamental pleasure. It is the opposite of loneliness. It is certainty. It is trust. It is kindness. It is fun. It is beyond age. It is incest without stigma.

I was once asked to define in print my idea of paradise. Sydney Smith defined his, you may remember, as 'eating pâté de foie gras to the sound of trumpets', a pleasure I could never share because of what they do to the geese. Mine was to be bowling across Castile in the Rolls-Royce Silver Dawn I had in those days, with the roof open, Mendelssohn on the radio and my Abyssinian cat beside me on the front seat. A reader promptly wrote to say that though he agreed about the place, the car, and possibly the music, he would want beside him something a lot more interesting than a cat.

He misunderstood my requirements. I did not want a sexual partner there. I did not want an expert on Spanish agriculture, I wanted a friend: a companion sensual in his presence, perhaps, but mostly silent, sufficiently elegant to match the landscape and the mascot on the front of the car, tactful enough not to interrupt the flow of the wind and the violins. I wanted someone constant, dependable and undemanding. If the cat purred I would not object, but I wanted no oohs and aahs out of him, only affectionate compliance with my mood, in return for my acceptance of his.

Friendship is a complementary quality, filling in gaps, patching cracks, soothing the orgiastic and jollying along the sluggish. It can be noisy indeed, it can be reckless and challenging; but it can also be sleepy and considerate on the front seat of the car, gently twitching its whiskers now and then, as a stork swoops down to a belfry nest, or a brown weasel scuttles into the ditch.

A snag about love is that it can so easily curdle into hate. Just as you can be tortured equally, they tell me, with ice-cold water or with boiling hot, so the love-hate relationship is not just a psychiatric cliché, but an emotional common-place. Like hate, love springs out in jerks and contradictions. Love is summoned by particular stimuli, sexual, tactile, olfactory, allusive, nostalgic, even digestatory. A hint of some sweet smell, the line of a melody, a smile perhaps, a more than usually ethereal zabaglione and suddenly for no more rational cause you are in each other's arms. Love is a creature of impulse, of fantasy and of fanaticism. It is the love of God, we are assured, that burns down upon us. It is for love of country that men die. Love hastens us all to excess, of good or evil. Love is extreme. Love lies. Love cheats. All's fair in love and war. Love is like a red, red rose.

How different are the evocations of friendship! The Quakers chose their works well, when they called themselves the Society of Friends, for friendship is traditionally reasonable, decent and restrained. Patriots feel love for their own country, but friendship for another; for the one they do heroic deeds, with the other they agree to limit imports of frozen ox-liver. The word 'friend', says the Oxford Dictionary, 'is not ordinarily applied to lovers or relatives', and this is because our feelings towards lovers, as towards relatives, are anything but reasonable, decent or restrained – we are given our relatives, as the saying goes, but thank God we can choose our friends!

Friendship is a premeditative condition – there is no such thing as a *crime d'amitié*. The Bible writers often mean friendship when they speak of love (surely it is friendship we really need of God), but Jesus picked his terms carefully, I am sure, when he spoke of laying down your life for your friends; not for your flaming lovers, not for your mothers and fathers – not in the sudden passion of the moment, either, in some flamboyant gesture of sacrifice – but steadily, thoughtfully, laying down a life as you might lay a carefully chosen gift.

The trouble is, friendship can be a bit of a bore. Friends can be bores themselves, Heaven knows. Even that cat of mine is a bore sometimes – 'Why can't you say something?' I sometimes hiss at

189

him, as he just sits there looking friendly. On the whole the tag about friends and relatives seems to me misguided, for I far prefer most of my relatives to most of my friends. My heart never sinks when, proclaiming a mighty appetite or an immediate need for hard cash, a child of mine bursts unexpectedly into the house: but dear God, does X really have to ring me *quite* so often for that friendly evening chat?

What one needs, then, is friendship spiked with passion. Walter Savage Landor thought the most delightful condition of all was 'a middle state between love and friendship', but I think love and friendship fused is best – of all human relationships, the most truly exciting. It must however be illuminated by lust – lust not necessarily of the body, but of the perceptions. Without lust of one sort or another, in my view, friendship drags. Fortunately I have shared my own life with a partner whose kind of friendship has been distinctly lustful (I am not now, of course, speaking of that cat). There is no kind of intimacy that we have not experienced over the years. We have procreated together. We have brought up children. We have spent long periods apart from one another, and long periods in the same room. We have exasperated each other, and thrown things at each other across kitchens. We have met each other in ecstasy after separations, and just occasionally, I dare say, been happy enough to say goodbye to each other.

A friendship like this, volatile though it may be, can never turn to hate, for it does not depend upon stimuli. It is complete in itself. It is self-energized. DYMA MAE DWY FFRIND, it says on the tombstone that already stands in my library, AR DERFYN UN BYWYD – HERE ARE TWO FRIENDS, AT THE END OF ONE LIFE. The best of all friendships are the ones that have ripened, over the long years, out of youth's carnality: keeping, when the blood grows colder, the fires of love alive.

36
Epilogue:
On Pleasure and Happiness

Plato and Socrates were right, I find: serious as pleasures are, they are insufficient by themselves. This is how Jack Fisher put it:

> Four Things for a Big Life
> 1 A great Inspiration
> 2 A great Cause
> 3 A great Battle
> 4 A great Victory

Without a battle, no victory: but not being an Admiral of the Fleet, I would rather say that pleasures must be flavoured with the salt of sorrow, before they amount to happiness.